# IRAQ

## FROM ADAM TO SADDAM

John Freeman

Pen Press

© John Freeman 2010

All rights reserved

No part of this publication may be reproduced, stored in a retrieval system, or transmitted in any form or by any means, without the prior permission in writing of the publisher, nor be otherwise circulated in any form of binding or cover other than that in which it is published and without a similar condition including this condition being imposed on the subsequent purchaser.

First published in Great Britain by Pen Press

All paper used in the printing of this book has been made from wood grown in managed, sustainable forests.

ISBN13: 978-1-907499-52-4

Printed and bound in the UK
Pen Press is an imprint of Indepenpress Publishing Limited
25 Eastern Place
Brighton
BN2 1GJ

A catalogue record of this book is available from the British Library

Cover design by Jacqueline Abromeit

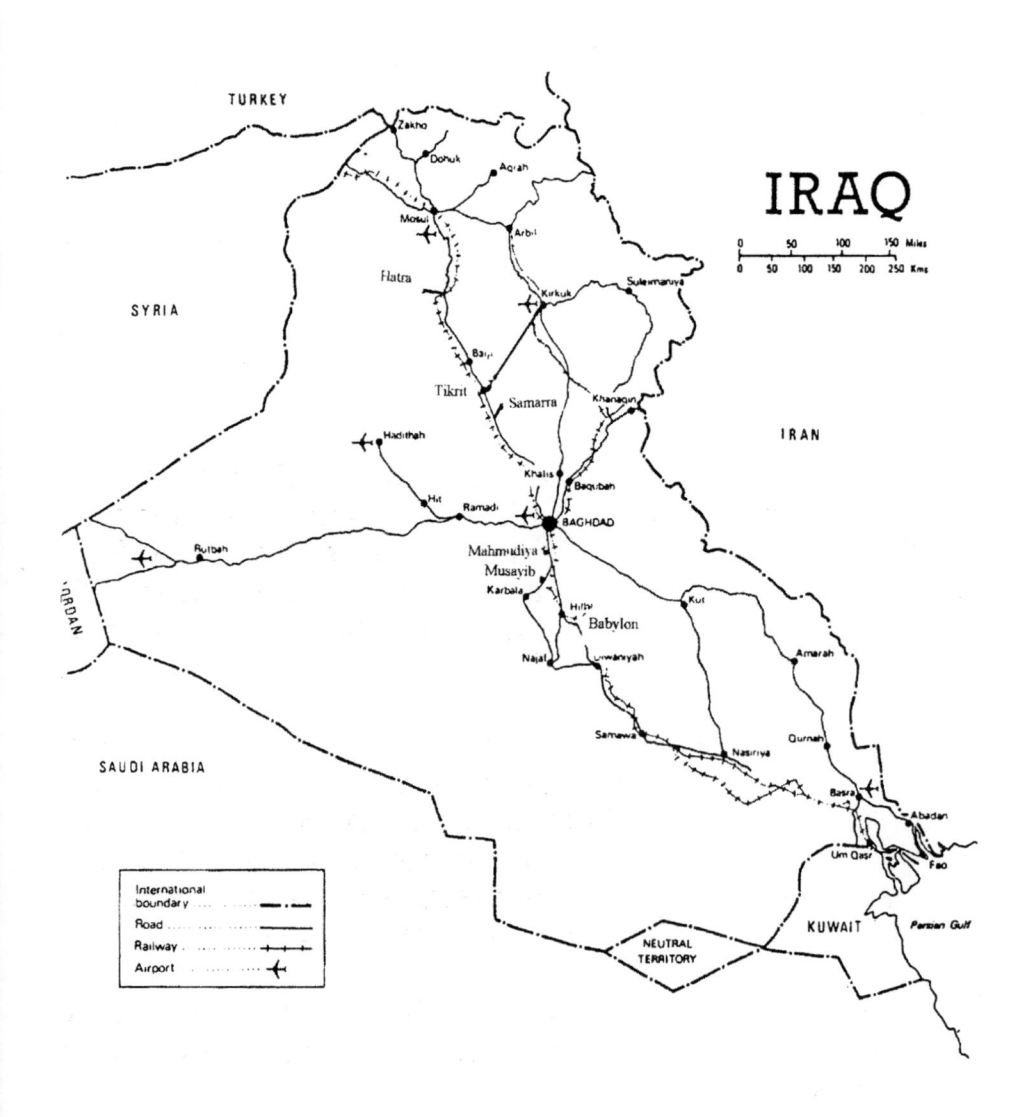

# IRAQ – FROM ADAM TO SADDAM

## FOREWORD

Dear Reader,

If I were to mention the country Iraq to you as I write in 2008, I guess that the first images that come into your mind would be scenes of chaos and destruction, also thousands of American troops in Baghdad and surrounding areas, and of British soldiers in Basrah.

Almost daily we heard of the deaths of US, or British personnel and of suicide bombings in crowded markets and the resulting bloodshed and ongoing grief of the Iraqi people. The TV pictures show it in detail but, in a way, we became immune to it all, regardless of the thousands of deaths that have occurred.

Likewise, there can't be many in the Western world who have not heard the name of Saddam Hussein. How many leaders of the other Middle Eastern states can you name? Not many I guess. Saddam Hussein is right up there with other monster dictators of the 20th century and has rightly been vilified and in the end been punished for his evil deeds.

All in all, Iraq is now identified with all that is wrong in the world. Saddam left a legacy of fear, religious and political rivalry with the ever present threat of civil war. To the outside world the situation appears almost insoluble. Considerable efforts have been made and elections have taken place but just as some calm has been achieved, some terrible action takes place, destroying the peace.

The purpose of this book is to show you that there is another side to Iraq, one which offers hope, and shows the Iraqi people in a more positive way.

I visited Iraq 37 times between 1975 and 1990. During this time I worked with companies from Mosul in the north to Basrah in the far south and my experiences have given me a good insight into the character of the people. I have nothing but admiration for the way in which they built up their manufacturing businesses and so improved the standard of living of ordinary Iraqis before they were so cruelly let down. In the 15 years I visited I could only watch as the companies were betrayed by Saddam's greed for power and after 1990 they were further let down by the United Nations – American led – and their policy of sanctions which hurt only the ordinary Iraqi people and not Saddam. Sadly the UK backed this policy.

My comments are in no way intended to criticise British or American forces. The politicians have given them an impossible job to do, and it is they who should carry the blame for the mess that Iraq now finds itself in. The sooner **all** troops are withdrawn, the more likely a solution will be found. Iraqis are not stupid, far from it and I firmly believe that they would find a compromise that would be acceptable to all.

After all, Iraq is sitting on oil reserves second only to those of Saudi Arabia, so has the potential to recover quickly. Iraqis are more than capable of running their own industries and do not need outside management.

As a people, I found them welcoming, honest, hard working and incredibly hospitable. In no way do I claim to be an expert on Iraq but can only tell it as I saw it. I made many friends during my visits and would love to go back one day.

I will try to weave into my narrative a sense of the history of this fascinating country and tell you about historical connections going back to the start of civilisation itself.

> "Where have all the flowers gone?
> Long time passing.
> Where have all the flowers gone?
> Long time ago.
> Where have all the flowers gone?
> Gone to graveyards every one.
> When will they ever learn?
> When will they ever learn!"
> ~~~~~~
> (Pete Seeger & Joe Hickerson)

# 1

## FROM ADAM TO SADDAM

Perhaps the first thing one should remember is that Iraq is a relatively new country, but one whose roots go back to the birth of civilisation itself.

The biggest influence on the way the country developed is the river systems, which run from north to south. The two great rivers, Euphrates and Tigris are as well known as say the Nile or Amazon.

The route of these rivers, through basically desert regions, has for many centuries defined the prosperity of the peoples living in the cities, towns and villages alongside, and for centuries have been the scene of countless wars as nearby tribes fought for control over the fertile lands.

The Euphrates is the most westerly of the two rivers. Its name is derived from the Greek meaning 'fruitful' or 'fertilising'. It rises in Syria as a result of several smaller rivers and combines with more sources as it flows through Turkey. Once it reaches Iraq, it has no other tributaries and flows south until it joins with the Tigris north of Basrah to form the Shatt al Arab Delta and then on to the Arabian Gulf.

Both the Euphrates and the Tigris are referred to in the Bible where the Garden of Eden is described in the Book of Genesis and the story of Adam and Eve began.

The Tigris, however, rises in Turkey and is a much faster flowing river than the Euphrates. Its name again has a Greek origin literally meaning 'tiger', reflecting the fierceness of the river flow. Once it joins with the Euphrates at Qurna to form the Shatt al Arab, it is still a further 100 miles before the Arabian Gulf is reached. According to legend, Qurna is the site of the Garden of Eden and there is a very ancient tree there, called Adam's tree.

Also in this area are the marshes where for countless generations the local people have lived on man-made islands constructed from a combination of earth, papyrus leaves, reeds and bulrushes. Their dwellings are similarly made and they and their animals co-exist in a way of life which stretches back into the mists of time.

An attempt was made by Saddam Hussein to have these marshes drained. This was partially successful but now the area is to be restored to its former state so that the remaining people can once again follow their previous way of life.

Fifty miles further south is Basrah. It was Iraq's main port but, being still 50 miles from the open sea, had restricted access to larger ships. It was not until the late 70s that a container port was built at Um Qasr. Basrah is the centre of the date growing area and the river banks contain many plantations and millions of date palms. It was from Basrah that Sinbad set out on his adventures.

From north to south is around 1,000km or 600 miles, so it is not surprising to find a great variation in climate along the way. The mountainous regions in the north bordering Turkey have long winters with plenty of snow, and its summers are dry and only moderately warm. Central and southern Iraq are semi-tropical and in high summer temperatures can reach 50ºc with 100% humidity in the Shatt al Arab region.

Looking at a map of the whole region from Syria to Iran it is the river Jordan in the west and the Euphrates and Tigris in the east that provide the life blood for their peoples and history records their struggle to keep control and repel invaders.

Some 10,000 archaeological sites have revealed just how civilisation grew and were the source of sciences that we take for granted today. There is evidence that 8,000 years ago a system of agricultural farming was in place, and skills in weaving, pottery and sculpture had been acquired.

Five thousand two hundred years ago the earliest form of writing had been developed and by 2371BC the land between the two rivers had been occupied by a people called the Akkadians – early Arab nationals – and their area of influence stretched from Syria to Iran.

The fertile nature of the land between the two rivers led to invasions from Persia [Iran] who were in turn conquered by the Sumerians around 3500BC. They were joined by the Semites, and the two groups gradually intermixed over many, many years and by 1750BC a king named Hammuradi established a capital called Babylon.

This empire lasted to around 1400BC when the Assyrians took over. They were skilled fighters and hunters and were the first to use horses. They built cities along the rivers such as Ninevah [now Mosul] in the north but the capital was kept at Babylon in the south. This was further developed by King Nebuchadnezzar. His workforce consisted of Jewish slaves captured during the Assyrian conquest of Palestine. The Bible records the despair of the slaves who were forced to turn Babylon into a magnificent city. They were kept in exile until the Assyrians were overthrown by King Cyrus' Persian army and were then allowed to return home, or at least those who had survived did. Once home those who had practised skills in transforming Babylon turned their attention to restoring the great temple in Jerusalem.

The Persians held the territory from 538 to 331BC and then it was the turn of Alexander the Great as the Greeks expanded their empire eastwards. It was now that the region became known as Mesopotamia although strictly speaking the translation "the land between two rivers" applied only to the area between the Euphrates and the Tigris.

The Greeks kept control until 135BC when the Persians regained the area and held it until 637AD. The Greeks however had benefited from the architectural knowledge gained from Babylon, and also Hatra in the north, and applied the same techniques when building Athens and in particular the Parthenon.

By this time the various Arab tribes were getting organised among themselves and were able to repel invaders and make the area their own. The Arab peoples welcomed the advent of Islam and this is reflected in the mosques established in this period.

Baghdad, by comparison with other places in Iraq, is relatively modern. It was founded in 762AD by Caliph Al Mansour, and it became a renowned centre of the arts and culture. There is also evidence of the beginnings of medicine, chemistry, geometry, mathematics, astronomy and poetry. All had their origins in this era.

After almost 500 years of Arab rule, the area was once again invaded this time by the Mongol hordes in 1258. They left a trail of destruction and horror from which the region could not recover. The Arab tribes had been scattered far and wide and were unable or unwilling to regroup.

This was the darkest of periods in Arab history and by the 16th century the Turkish Ottoman Empire had expanded to take in the land. Baghdad however remained at the crossroads of the ancient caravan routes bringing spices and silks from the Far East on their way to Europe. Whilst Baghdad continued to prosper, the rest of the area declined steadily.

Turkish control was to remain until the 1914-18 war when the Turks sided with Germany. Britain saw this as a threat to their Indian interests and a force was despatched from India to Basrah to establish a base there. In order to drive the Turks out, the British needed the co-operation of the local Arab tribes. They had well armed militias but were frequently at odds with each other.

In 1916 two spheres of action were launched. The first was organised from Cairo where the British had their command base, this saw the exploits of Lawrence of Arabia. He enlisted the support of Prince Faisal of Saudi Arabia whose army joined with other tribes to drive the Turks first out of Saudi Arabia, then Palestine and finally getting their surrender in Damascus.

The other force, which had been sent from India, had instructions to push north from Basrah with the aim of capturing Baghdad. They were badly equipped and ill prepared for the task. They used the two rivers to establish bases along the route but did not attract the same level of support from the local tribes and as a consequence were usually outnumbered by the Turks. Also the climate played a big part and disease killed as many as were killed in action.

The British almost reached Baghdad but had to pull back to Kut where after a long siege they had no option but to surrender. It was an ignominious chapter in British military history, although there were many acts of heroism.

The success of Lawrence and Faisal however made it impossible for the Turks to stay in the region, and it was left to the British and French to decide the future of the whole area. Faisal had been promised along with other Arab leaders that they would be given complete control in exchange for their support. When it came to the final negotiations however they found that the British and French had no intention of relinquishing control. Behind the scenes, diplomats from Britain and France had reached an agreement to carve up the region between them. This was known as the Sykes-Picot agreement after the names of the two main officials.

It was no surprise therefore that Faisal and the other Arab leaders felt betrayed and threatened further strife if their demands for self rule were not met. A peace conference was hurriedly arranged in Paris in 1919 and Faisal led the Arab delegation. A compromise solution was partially accepted in that various emirates or kingdoms would be established throughout the former Ottoman Empire. Faisal, a direct descendant of the Prophet Mohammed, was declared King of Syria on March 7$^{th}$ 1920.

The French however were not happy with the Paris agreement and at a second conference in San Remo, invoked the original Sykes-Picot plan. France took over control of Syria and Lebanon and Faisal was expelled and came to London. There was now considerable unrest in Mesopotamia as a result of the Anglo French policy and a quick resolution was needed to prevent further conflict.

The British Government decided against direct rule in Iraq, proposing a monarchy. A plebiscite was held which showed that 96% of the local tribal chiefs approved of Faisal and in 1921 he was declared King of Iraq on 23$^{rd}$ August.

Britain maintained its mandate over the territory with the approval of The League of Nations. Postage stamps issued from 1918 to 1921 were Turkish stamps overprinted with the words 'IRAQ IN

BRITISH OCCUPATION.' What a start to so-called independence! Faisal however was no puppet king, and continually pushed for a truly independent Arab nation, and by 1924 an assembly had been formed to establish a permanent form of government.

Vast oil reserves were found in the early 20s and this gave Faisal terrific bargaining power. A concession was given to an internationally owned oil company to develop these reserves, and in 1927, the first oil was pumped. In the same year Faisal asked for British support for Iraq's application to join The League of Nations and end the British mandate.

At first Britain refused, mindful of the rich pickings from oil revenue. Faisal did not give up and continually pushed the British Government. Eventually a Treaty of Friendship was signed between Iraq and Britain, and as a result Britain backed Iraq's application, and in 1932, Iraq became a fully independent sovereign state. Faisal however only lived 12 months more and died in 1933.

He was succeeded by his son Ghazi, but he was killed in a mysterious road accident in 1939, and was succeeded in turn by his son Faisal II. As he was only 3 at the time of the succession, his uncle Abd al – Ilah ruled as regent until Faisal came of age in 1953.

The Second World War put paid temporally to Arabian ambitions and Iraq became an important staging post for British forces bound for India and the Far East. A huge base at Habbaniya north of Baghdad employed hundreds of Iraqi personnel.

After the war finished, the desire to have total control over oil production returned and became a major political issue with the majority wanting all foreign participation ended. There was however a small but powerful minority who wanted to maintain the link to the West.

The establishment of the State of Israel pushed this issue to the back temporally, and the Arab Nations were thrown into turmoil, all vowing to drive the Israelis into the sea. Syria and Egypt led by the charismatic Gamal Nasser agreed to form a United Arab Republic. Iraq and Jordan decided to form an Arab Federation with Faisal II at its head.

The federation was short lived for on the 14th July 1958, Col. Abdul Karim Qassim led a coup d'etat. The whole royal family was ordered into the palace courtyard and executed by a firing squad. The prime minister, Nuri as Said was murdered the next day. It was thought that this coup was brought about as a result of pressure from the newly formed United Arab Republic and which was very much anti West whereas Jordan and Iraq were perceived to be pro West.

The new regime immediately cancelled its Treaty of Friendship with Britain, known as the Baghdad Pact. The turmoil in Iraq was far from over. Between 1958 and 1968 a further three coups took place. After the final one, Major General Ahmed Hassan al Bakr was declared President and Saddam Hussein, the Secretary of the Iraq Baath Socialist Party was named as Vice President.

In 1968 Saddam Hussein was 31. He was born near Tikrit, a small town north of Baghdad on the road to Mosul. The name 'Saddam' in Arabic means "One who confronts". He studied law for three years before dropping out of the course, and joining the Baath Party to assist with administration. He was greatly influenced by his uncle, Kharqillah Tulfah and quickly worked his way up to become secretary of the party. Involved in one of the earlier coups, he had spent some time living in exile and had been a keen observer of the end of monarchies in Egypt and Libya. Arab nationalism was very much in the ascendancy, and Saddam was ready to play his part.

The above is only a brief summary of how Iraq evolved. Great scholars have written many books on the subject, and my account does not really do justice to the history, but I hope it has served to show you that over thousands of years, "The land between two rivers" has been continually fought over by non Arabs trying to protect self interests, whether it be water, strategic bases and finally oil.

As an independent State, Iraq is, by comparison with most countries, a new country still evolving and with a lot of difficulties still to face. Its history over thousands of years is dominated by a common theme – **occupation**. There has rarely been a time when the area has not been the target of some outside power. It is little wonder then that any sort of "occupation" whether well intended or not, is seen as an infringement of national liberty. The Americans, British and other forces will have to leave one day and it will be a real test of the Iraqi people to try and move on from this dreadful period in their history.

King Faisal. Note Indian currency

King Ghazi

King Faisal II

General Kassem – Leader of 1958 coup

9

President Al Bakr

President Saddam Hussein

# 2

## "AT HARRODS WE DO NOT HAGGLE"

As a boy, I was taken to see the film *The Thief of Baghdad* starring Douglas Fairbanks. It was a film full of colour, drama and spectacular sword fights. I had also read stories of *Ali Baba and the Forty Thieves* as well as Sinbad's voyages and *1001 Nights, Stories of Scheherazade*, and so had a very romantic vision of Iraq.

I was also a keen stamp collector and my album contained early issues showing King Faisal. After leaving school I was employed by one of Europe's leading packaging companies and after spending two years in the production offices I got a job as a sales correspondent in the export section of the company. This was in the late 50s when overseas travel was very limited, and business was done by letter. No e-mail, fax or telex, and overseas phone calls had to be booked well in advance!

We had a customer in Basrah who had a date plantation and bought "Cellophane" wrappers from us printed with a design called "Black Swan." There followed a huge order from the Iraqi Date Board for wrappers bearing brand names such as Lion of Babylon, Camel and Sinbad. These products were intended for the UK market and Europe. They recognised that the packaging had to be of a certain standard in order to compete with the boxed dates coming from North Africa. Packs would be in 4oz, 6oz and 1lb blocks. One of the problems was that the stickiness of the dates affected the print but we overcame the problem by printing a metallic gold or silver base and the design on top.

Orders had to be shipped by the middle of August, so as to reach Basrah by early September when the packing season began. The finished product was then shipped back to the UK and Europe in time to benefit from the Christmas market.

The 60s were an even more turbulent time for Iraq. After the monarchy had been so brutally despatched in 1958, the struggle between the various army and Baath party activists resulted in three further coups and some sort of stability was not achieved until 1968 when Saddam Hussein was appointed deputy to President Al Bakr.

We started to become aware of major developments in the Middle East in the early 70s. Saudi Arabia and the Yemen Arab Republic were encouraging local production of food products normally imported from Europe. These included sweets and biscuits, which required our type of packaging.

Our sales force did not have time to devote to this area and I found myself dealing with all the business, albeit at first in the UK. At a packaging exhibition in London in 1973, I was contacted by an Iraqi businessman, Mr Jumaili, who owned a biscuit factory in Baghdad. I had already written to him with an offer and now he wanted to finalise his order. We occupied a small cubicle in the exhibition hall and I was immediately informed that our offer was too expensive. This was my first experience of "negotiating" Middle East style. I knew what margin I had to play with, which wasn't much, so in order to protect it I gradually got Mr Jumaili to increase the quantity so reducing our production costs. The negotiations took the best part of an hour during which Mr Jumaili had several times raised his voice because of my reluctance to drop the price even further, but finally he accepted the revised offer. He was happy and so was I, having maintained the original profit margin. Such had been the noise level coming from the cubicle that I discovered it had been quite an entertainment for eavesdroppers!

Our parent company were by this time supplying large quantities of unprinted material to large State owned companies in Iraq producing cigarettes and also pharmaceuticals. They had appointed an agent to help promote their business, and it made sense for us to use the same agent. His name was Leon Sarkis, a man in his 60s. The strange thing was that, initially, we took an instant dislike of each other although we eventually became great friends. He accused us of being slow to respond to enquiries, not realising that the costing of printed material was far more complicated than that for unprinted.

In 1974 I had visited the Yemen Arab Republic and also Saudi Arabia and business from these areas was developing nicely. The level of enquiries from Iraq was still fairly low, however one day in February 1975, I received a telephone call from an office in London with a request to come that day to meet an Iraqi businessman who wanted to place a large order.

I took a train around lunchtime from Bristol to London and arrived at the office in Sloane Square in good time. There I was introduced to Abdul Wahab Al Bunnia, an imposing figure in full Arab dress. I could not guess his age because he was quite scarred around the face and had suffered some damage to his right hand. I learnt later that he had been badly burned in an accident as a boy. Although his English was very good, he left it to his London office manager to tell me what he was looking for and it was for 20 tons of printed packaging for his new biscuit factory in Baghdad. My problem was that it had to be shipped in less than five weeks. I knew the costs involved and after a short negotiation [short by Jumaili standards!] we agreed a deal. I learnt that the Iraqi Government were encouraging local production initiatives and readily granting licences and loans for all sorts of projects and in particular those covering food.

With this encouragement, Iraqi businessmen were coming to Europe to buy machinery, and in our case packaging, for the production of biscuits, sweets, chocolate and snack foods. I was getting a lot of information from machine companies in the UK, Germany and Switzerland, and another visit from Leon Sarkis convinced us that a trip to Iraq could pay off.

Many Iraqis came to London and opened offices, usually manned by a member of the family. During the summer, many came with their families to escape the 50°c temperatures in Baghdad and I heard a story that one of the teenage sons of one businessman went shopping at Harrods. The father received a telephone call from the Harrods manager asking him to speak to his son and to tell him that "At Harrods we do not haggle!"

To get an Iraqi visa required an invitation from a State owned company but this presented no problem as we already had contact with the pharmaceutical company in Samarra. We had shipped the Bunnia order in time, so the plan was to go to Baghdad after its arrival and to negotiate further business.

# 3

## NEMO REPENTE FUIT TURPISSIMUS Juvenal AD60
### Trans. NO ONE EVER BECAME THOROUGHLY BAD ALL AT ONCE

On the 11th April 1975 I departed for Baghdad. There were no direct flights from the UK then, and I went via Beirut. Arriving at Baghdad airport at nearly midnight I found the place crowded with Egyptians all waiting to complete immigration procedures. Since none of them had completed the landing cards, I knew I was in for a long wait and it was two hours before I finally emerged into the arrivals hall and was very relieved to find Leon Sarkis waiting for me. He took me to a small hotel in Saadoun Street and said he would collect me in the morning.

Next day, the first thing I wanted to do was to let my wife know that I had arrived safely, so Leon took me to the central post office in the heart of the business area. I was immediately struck by the crowds intermingling with heavy traffic, and there seemed to be a tremendous energy around. This transferred into the postal building but somehow we manoeuvred ourselves to a counter and I gave a short message to the clerk. He wrote it down in Arabic so I did wonder how it would arrive in Bristol. I need not have worried for I found out on my return that it came correctly the same morning. We paid the appropriate charge and left.

The next port of call was the duty free shop, which was quite near. People arriving from abroad could buy duty free goods here up to 24 hours after arrival. I did not want anything, but Leon was keen to use me to get a bottle of whisky. The building was packed with long queues and I resigned myself to a long wait. To my astonishment Leon guided me to the top of the queue and placed the order. No one objected, not even a mild protest, and when I asked Leon why not, he said that everyone in the queue was Egyptian and if they had made any sort of protest they would have been in trouble

We then drove to Leon's office/factory in the suburbs. Nice wide streets but plenty of traffic with much use of the horn in evidence. On the way I noticed streets of nice flat topped white houses with pleasant colourful gardens. The office was a nondescript building and a poster was pasted on the wall of the entrance with photographs of President Al Bakr and Vice President Saddam Hussein.

Leon's office was a simple affair with two desks, one for him and the other for his business partner. A few chairs and filing cabinets completed the scene as well as photographs of the President and Vice President on the wall. Leon's main business was the selling of adhesive tape. They had an exclusive deal with the UK's largest tape manufacturer and also imported jumbo reels, which were slit down in a small factory unit behind the office. Judging by the number of people coming in to office, they were obviously very successful. Everyone was offered tea in one of the small glass cups, which I was to become very familiar with.

I was itching to get going but Leon was in no hurry, and it was late morning before we set off for my first meeting. The trip took us through more suburbs and I could not help noticing the number of construction sites. The skyline seemed dominated by tall cranes. We had crossed the Tigris on one of several bridges and passed many government buildings and parks. We also passed the now infamous Abu Ghraib prison and arrived at the factory around midday. This company made high quality chocolate all packed in very ornate boxes. Leon told me that the company was owned by Christians and was very well respected. I was well received and took details of possible items that would interest our company, but I got the strong impression that they did not expect to see me again.

Leon then had to visit one of his customers in central Baghdad and we parked in Rashid Street, one of the main thoroughfares, and walked into the bazaar area known as the Shorja. This was an amazing place. With the temperature up in the high 80s we entered a system of narrow alleyways. The area was heaving mass of humanity, all pushing their way through. To add to the general chaos were porters carrying huge loads on their backs or someone leading a packhorse. The alleys were much too narrow for any vehicle traffic. Once I'd adjusted to my surroundings, I noticed that the market operated on a labyrinth system with each arm offering a particular product, so the spice, vegetable, cloth, hardware, gold and silver merchants, all had their own alleys. The noise levels were tremendous, especially in the tin/copper market where men and boys were hammering out pots, pans and ornate decorative plates depicting Iraq's historical sites.

We made our way right into the heart of the Shorja, and located Leon's customer who ran a stationery store. The layout was extremely cramped with shelves containing paper products rising to at least 12 feet high. As it was now lunchtime we sat on wooden stools eating kebabs and drinking tea in the glass cups. There were many sources of food and drink in the market and boys carrying tea seemed to be everywhere. I found the whole place fascinating and over the years never tired of walking through it.

As we travelled back to my hotel we passed yet more construction sites. New roads, flyovers, office/apartment blocks were in hand, and this was where the guest workers from Egypt were being employed. Baghdad had surprised me on first impressions. It certainly wasn't like stepping back in time as it was in the Yemen.

It was the practice for businesses to close around 2 o'clock and reopen around 6, so Leon dropped me off at the hotel and said he would come back later. My room had been cleaned but I was aware that my case had been searched. Nothing was missing but it made me a little wary. I mentioned it to Leon when he came for me and he told me that all the hotels were government owned and that there was some anti-West feeling because of the Israeli situation.

From a small bookstall near the hotel, I had bought a copy of an English language newspaper, The Baghdad Observer. There was no international news and it was full of reports about the RCC, the Revolutionary Command Council, a group of 26 who effectively ran the country. There appeared to be several conferences attended by foreign delegations, all of whom had been greeted by the Vice President, Saddam Hussein. There was little mention of the President Hassan Al Bakr.

The politics of the whole region were very unsettled. Iraq seemed at odds with all its neighbours; with Syria over the damming of the Euphrates causing low water flow in the agricultural areas, with Jordan over the Palestinian refugee crisis, with Iran over the control of the Shatt Al Arab Delta, with Kuwait over border issues and finally Turkey regarding a problem with the Kurds.

I met with Leon in the evening to try and plan the next day and after a meal had an early night to catch up with sleep lost the night before. I normally can get to sleep quickly but the impressions of the day kept going round my mind and the noise of the crickets outside was very loud and persistent.

The next day did not start well. Leon met me in his rather battered old Renault. He told me that the waiting list for a new car was well over 12 months, and then only if you were lucky. We had only gone a few yards when the car engine died and we stopped. Leon could not restart the engine. We were still in Saadoun Street, one of Baghdad's busiest thoroughfares, so there was much horn blowing by passing traffic. Soon quite a crowd gathered round. No AA or RAC here! Among the onlookers were several boys so Leon persuaded eight of them to push the car and try and jump start it with no success. There was nothing for it but to leave the car and take a taxi to Leon's office.

This really screwed up the day and no calls were possible as Leon frantically phoned round trying to find a garage to collect and fix his car. Eventually he was successful and had a call very late in the afternoon to say it had been fixed, but it was too late to make any visits.

Leon had invited me to his house that evening for a meal and this was to be a real education. There I met his wife Asdigh and three of his five sons. The other two were in Europe studying at university. They all had or were studying different professions and I got the impression that they were being groomed to run a Sarkis business sometime in the future.

I was made very welcome and started to find out about the family background. The Sarkis family had originated in Armenia and like many other families had fled the country after the Russian revolution. They first settled in Basrah, but moved to Baghdad after the Second World War. Here, there was already a large Armenian community, and even a church following the Orthodox line. They had had a small stationery business but Leon decided to set himself up as a commission agent when Iraq started to develop in the 60s. Although commission agents generally were frowned upon, the tape and packaging business was providing a good source of income, and Leon, with his previous contacts, appeared well respected. Anticipating that the Iraq Government might at some stage ban the importation of tape in favour of local production, Leon had acquired land on which he intended to build his own factory. He had already acquired a licence to produce tape so his future looked secure.

The meal started around 9pm and some dishes were brought out and a plate piled high with still warm, flat, unleavened Arab bread. The dishes contained various dips of houmas, chick peas, tabullah and a plate of dolma which is a mixture of rice and minced meat stuffed into a rolled vine leaf. I tucked in thinking that this was the main meal. It was all very tasty. I should have known better as this was only the starter. The main course was Masgouf, a large fish cooked whole and presented on a large metal platter. One of the sons had collected it from the cookhouses in Abu Nawas Street alongside the river Tigris.

Leon had called there on his way to pick me up. The system was that you selected the size of fish you wanted from the ones swimming around a large tank. They are caught in the Tigris and put live into the tanks. Selection is based on how many people are coming to dinner. Some of the larger fish could feed a dozen people and would cost £150. The fish are cooked over an open sandalwood fire with the fish opened up and spread over a metal frame. The seller knows how long it will take to cook and gives the buyer a time to collect.

It is served with tomatoes, onions and the flat bread. It has to be eaten using fingers as there are many bones, but the fish was marvellous, quite unlike anything I had tasted before. I was given a slice of lemon to rub over my hands afterwards.

That was not the end of the meal for plates of Arab sweetmeats appeared containing Baclawa, a combination of crushed pistachio nuts, honey and syrup. Also Manna, a nougat type confection containing pistachio nuts.

By the time Leon took me back to the hotel I knew I had eaten too much and had been quite overwhelmed with the hospitality. There was no way I was going to get to sleep quickly so I wrote a letter to my wife. It began:-

"Midnight and I've just got back from the agent's house where I've had a rather large meal [understatement] so its going to be an hour or so before I feel like hitting the pillow"

On day three we had to go to Samarra to the factory of the State Drug Company who had issued the necessary invitation to enable me to get a visa. We took the main road north, down which came all the traffic from Mosul and Turkey. As we left the outer confines of Baghdad, we could see a huge road building project taking shape with several flyovers. The system was being built to provide a bypass to Baghdad to speed up traffic heading south particularly at Haj time when pilgrims were on their way to Mecca from Turkey and the north.

Samarra is about 75 miles from Baghdad and at first a dual carriageway made driving easy for Leon. We passed a large military base, heavily guarded and with 'NO PHOTOGRAPHY' signs in Arabic and English at regular intervals. However we were soon down to a single road with heavy traffic in both directions. It was dead straight as far as the eye could see and in the distance I could see a line of black smoke stretching across the horizon. As we got nearer I could see it was coming from a line of tall chimneys at a brick works. As we passed by I could see that oil was being used to fire the kilns, hence the black smoke. We had to keep the car windows shut because of the choking fumes. I was amazed to see that there were crude dwellings alongside the kilns and small children playing outside. It was a truly awful place but obviously some people's way of life.

Once past this place we were into a desert landscape, barren and treeless save for some scrub. The only signs of life were occasional flocks of sheep or goats being herded alongside the road. Each flock had a lead sheep or goat and I thought that this was the way they had been taken from one grazing area to another for hundreds of years. I would have loved to have stopped and taken a photograph but it was not possible.

The journey was becoming more dangerous as the road got narrower and the bumps and potholes more frequent. Heavy container lorries and fuel tankers were heading towards Baghdad and at times their overtaking was downright suicidal. We often passed debris from accidents on the side of the road.

The last few miles to Samarra were on a spur road, which took us past a large area of marshes with tall reeds. Perched on top were many pied kingfishers, a much bigger version of their European counterparts.

We had a successful visit to the pharmaceutical factory, which was important, as I needed their invitation to apply for a visa if I was coming back.

Samarra is an ancient town dating back to AD 836. Situated close to the Tigris, it was the capital of an area controlled by a Caliph Al – Mo'tassim. He built the largest mosque in the world at that time, and its walls are still standing. It was right next to the factory I'd just visited. Next to the ancient mosque was another unique structure. It was a ziggurat or staged tower in which each storey is smaller than the one below it. The top is reached by an outside stairway and I could see people climbing it.

Leon then took me to see the golden mosque, the holy shrine of Imam Ali al Hadi, which dated back to the 13th century. The roof is, or was, covered with a layer of pure gold, and it was possible to see the sun reflecting on it from 20 miles away. It is a shrine sacred to Shiite Moslems and sadly was destroyed early in 2007 by Sunni Moslems in revenge for attacks on their mosques. Much to Leon's surprise, a guard invited me into the mosque's courtyard to take some pictures but showed me a line on the ground, which I was not to cross.

The journey back to Baghdad was equally nerve wracking. Leon's Renault wasn't capable of great speed, and we frequently had great lorries tailgating us, horn blaring, before overtaking. I was glad to get back to the hotel in one piece!

Day four I had reserved for the Al Bunnia business. When in London, Mr Al Bunnia had made it quite clear that he would not deal through commission agents so I had to explain to Leon that this business had to be excluded from the agency. He wasn't surprised because he knew of Mr Al Bunnia and had told me how important a figure he was in the food manufacturing industry.

I took a taxi to the office in Jamhouriya Street in the heart of the business area. I went up a flight of stairs and saw Mr Al Bunnia sitting at his desk and he beckoned me to come straight in. I thought this was a good start, but over the next two hours realised that I had not been given any special treatment.

Having exchanged greetings, I sat on the opposite side of the desk and was given the customary sweet black tea. Whilst I sipped the tea a procession of people entered the office and came backwards and forwards to his desk with pieces of paper for him to sign or get instructions on something or other. It was clear that nothing was done without Mr Al Bunnia's say so. As the conversations were in Arabic, I didn't have a clue what was going on.

In between interruptions, Mr Al Bunnia gave me the background to the business. It had been started by his father as a food importing company but now the Iraqi Government's policy was to make the country self-sufficient and encouraging local production by banning imports of finished food products. Special licences had been issued for the purchase of machinery and for the biscuit factory Mr Al Bunnia had bought the best two biscuit lines from the UK and top of the range packaging machines from Switzerland.

Mr Al Bunnia had two brothers. Abdul Latif ran the financial side of the business, a very pleasant man who dressed western style as opposed to his brother. The other brother Saadoun lived abroad and handled some of the company's overseas business. I also met Mr Al Bunnia's clerk, Mr Shakir who was responsible for all the paperwork and correspondence. He too was very pleasant and asked me to bring him a good English dictionary next time I came, which I thought was an encouraging sign. Two of Mr Al Bunnia's sons, Khalid and Mohammed were being groomed to be part of the business. On the office wall were pictures of Mr Al Bunnia's father, President Al Bakr and Vice President Saddam Hussein.

After a couple of hours during which I only had half an hour of his attention and had drunk numerous glasses of tea, I was asked to go to the factories.

Transport was laid on, and I first went to the biscuit factory, which was where our material had been sent. Production was on the ground floor with raw materials being stored in a basement. I was concerned about the lack of air conditioning as our packaging could absorb moisture and become unusable. I noticed that the storage condition labels on the boxes were in English, which was a fat lot of good as the storekeeper couldn't read English. I made a note to get Arabic ones printed and used.

The production manager was an Austrian called Hubert Raudaschl who was being driven crazy by the "operators" of the two biscuit lines. He was trying to train them and at the same time maintain a good production rate. He appreciated my visit and I was able to give him some advice about storing and handling the packaging. I felt I would have an ally in him.

I then went to the nearby sweet and chewing gum factory, which was managed by Mr Al Bunnia's nephew Tariq. The place was well run and the equipment easier to use, and they had received technical assistance from Nestle and Dandy in Denmark whose products they were manufacturing under licence.

By now it was late afternoon and I returned to the Bunnia office to report my findings. I was then invited to Mr Al Bunnia's house that evening. From the hotel I phoned Leon and he warned me that the meal would not be a "simple" affair such as the one I'd had at his house!

I was collected from the hotel and taken to the Bunnia house in the Mansour district, which is where the "well to do" of Baghdad live. The family owned three large properties, which ran the whole length of the street. I was joined by a Swedish and Italian man. They were working in other factories owned by the family. Tea was provided and then we were shown into what I can only describe as Mr Al Bunnia's treasure room. It was full of ornaments gold and silver, ivory figures, paintings and etchings illustrating Arabic art and a collection of prayer beads.

The prize exhibit however was a pile of carpets in the middle of the room. They were neatly arranged and one of the sons pulled out examples to show us the intricate patterns that had been woven. The real challenge was to have two the same, because this increased the value considerably so we were told.

From the Sarkis experience I knew we wouldn't be eating very early, and sure enough it was 10 o'clock before were shown into the dining room. There I saw a long table with 14 place settings. The table was laden with food from one end to the other. Plates of beef, lamb, chicken, fish and dips of houmas, chick peas, tabullah and dolma. Whole roast chickens, and fresh fruits of every description. Finally plates of Arab cakes, baclawa and manna.

There was enough food for 40 never mind four, then we noticed that Mr Al Bunnia was not going to be eating but with two of his sons, was going to serve us. They stood at the end of the table waiting for their father's orders. We were not allowed to help ourselves and we were first given an assortment of the meats. They were very tender but one had only to say how nice it was and immediately another helping was put on the plate.

And so it went on. Soon the other two were complaining about weight problems so the portions did get smaller, all washed down with grapefruit juice. We asked if anyone else would be joining us in view of the number of place settings and it was explained to us that it is the Arab custom to lay extra places in case of unexpected visitors. An extra 11 seemed a touch over the top but I certainly felt privileged to experience such hospitality even though I'd probably eaten enough to last me a week!

So it was another late night and I had to be up at 4.30am to get a taxi to the airport as I was going to Basrah on the 6.00am flight. The flight was full, and we left on time, flying south between the Tigris and Euphrates. I could see the land was well cultivated but there were areas where the desert had taken over because the Euphrates had not flooded due to the Syrians reducing the flow by damming. Further south we passed over the marshes where the nomadic Marsh Arabs lived on the man made islands made of mud and reeds. There was talk of draining the marshes but it would be a terrible shame to deprive these people of their way of life. The Shatt Al Arab delta became visible and we descended into Basrah.

Security at Baghdad had been very tight, my camera had been taken away and I was told it would be handed back at Basrah. The reason for the security became clear because we had landed at a military airbase outside Basrah. Apparently the domestic airport was being renovated. A fleet of single decker buses painted all colours of the rainbow took us into Basrah. The road was full of potholes and I reckon our bus hit every one. We passed the oil terminals and the port area before arriving at the normal airport terminal building. 'NO PHOTOGRAPHY' signs in English and Arabic were everywhere.

I was met by a friend of Leon's, a Mr Zanontian, and after I had reclaimed my camera, he drove me to the date plantations which stretched for miles along the river banks. We stopped at a packing station run by a Mr Cyril Asfar who was an independent grower and not linked to the State owned company. His brand was Black Swan. He showed me the wooden blocks into which dates were compressed before wrapping. It seemed a very laborious process but there was no machinery to handle such a sticky product.

We had lunch at Mr Asfar's house. We were treated to another fish, a spiky looking thing called Zubaidy. It tasted good though. I was given a glass of white liquid, which I thought was milk but turned out to be liquid yoghurt, locally known as Laban. I managed to drink it, just! It is supposed to be good for digestive problems and give long life. Over the next few years I got to like it a lot and always had it when available, and I certainly believe the claim regarding indigestion!

As we came to leave, we heard a cat mewing underneath Mr Zanontian's car. We looked underneath and saw that the cat had given birth to three kittens. As we watched she carried them out one by one to some bushes on the side of the road.

My return to Baghdad followed the same pattern as the inward journey. Camera taken, same old buses and potholes, and tight security at the military airfield. It was getting dark as we flew north and it was even more noticeable how the towns and villages were built by the rivers and the empty spaces on the right and left. Thankfully there was no invitation to dinner that night so I was able to catch up on some sleep.

Day 6, Thursday was going to be my last working day as Friday is the weekend in the Moslem world and I was going on to Kuwait. I went to the Bunnia office early to clear up one or two matters and managed to have his full attention. Business was good and I said I would be back later in the year. I then met Leon and we drove to Hillah, some 20 miles south of Baghdad, to see a possible client. Before we returned, Leon took me to a historical site nearby. This was the Arch of Ctesiphon. Originally it was part of a palace built by the Parthian kings in the first century BC. It is said to be the largest arch made of bricks anywhere in the world. Another example of Iraq's fascinating history that I had seen in only a week. The best was still to come.

Coppersmith in Shorja

Coppersmith in Shorja

Copperware shop in the Shorja

Inside the Shorja Baghdad

Wedding cake shop

14th Ramadan Mosque Baghdad

Arab Dhow at Basrah

Date Palm inspection, Basrah

Approaching the brickworks

The Brickworks north of Baghdad

Golden Shrine of Imam Ali al Hadi Samarra

Malwiya spiral minaret Samarra

Al Bunnia Mosque, Baghdad

Abdul Wahab Al Bunnia

Masgouf fish

Masgouf being cooked

Cooking Masgouf

Masgouf ready to eat

Candle stall in the Shorja

Heavy load for a porter in the Shorja

Pack horse in the Shorja

Shopkeeper in the Shorja Baghdad

Coppersmith Shorja Baghdad

Narrow alley in the Shorja

# 4

## BY THE RIVERS OF BABYLON WE SAT DOWN
PSALM 137

Early on the Friday morning I received a call from the Bunnia office [open on a Friday!] asking if I would like to join a small group going to Babylon. My only reservation was would I be back in time to catch my evening flight to Kuwait? I was assured that I would be, so I didn't need asking twice.

I was picked up by a minibus, and joined five other Europeans including the Swede and Italian I had met two nights previously. It took 1½ hours to reach the site. As we travelled through flat, sun baked countryside south of Baghdad, it struck me that apart from the road, the area must be the same as it was when various armies of Persia, Alexander the Great and other conquering hordes invaded this part of the world centuries ago.

It was in 1899 that a German archaeologist, Robert Koldewey first started excavating a cluster of mounds near the river Euphrates. Slowly and painstakingly over the next 10 years he uncovered the ruins of Babylon, a city whose history goes back 4,000 years when Nebuchadnezzar fulfilled his ambition to build a beautiful city.

Nebuchadnezzar's empire stretched far to the north and west to the Mediterranean where he conquered Judah and captured Jerusalem. He needed a great workforce to carry out his ambitious plans for a magnificent capital city, so the Israelites were forced into exile at Babylon.

The Israelites lament is recorded in Psalm 137:-

"By the rivers of Babylon we sat down,
there we wept when we remembered Zion.

On the willows near by
we hung up our harps.
Those who captured us told us to sing;
They told us to entertain them:
"sing us a song about Zion"
How can we sing a song to the Lord in a foreign land?"

The Psalm ends with a note of defiance:-

"Babylon, you will be destroyed.
Happy is the man who pays you back
for what you have done to us"

Of course, like Rome, Babylon wasn't built in a day and was planned in careful stages, although it required regular repairs following frequent wars. It was finally destroyed by the Persians in 1530BC, and as it gradually crumbled, it was taken over by the desert until it was discovered in 1899.

From the ruins it has been possible to build up a picture of what the city was like and it must have been magnificent. The city walls were wide enough for a four-horse chariot to turn on, and these were the main defences.

High above everything else stood the Tower of Babel. Built as a square ziggurat with each section smaller than the one beneath. It is believed that there were seven levels, with a temple erected on the seventh. A huge staircase led to the second stage and the main entrance. A smaller staircase led to the first stage.

Buildings were constructed with thick walls and no windows. Nebuchadnezzar's Summer Palace had walls 20 feet thick to keep the rooms cool during the searing summer heat. All bricks used in the construction of Babylon were inscribed with Nebuchadnezzar's name so that his name would be forever remembered.

The main entrance to the city of Babylon was found partially intact and has been reconstructed. This gate, dedicated to the Goddess Ishtar, now dominates the entrance to the site and is adorned with bas reliefs of bulls and dragons, animals sacred to the Babylonians.

The entrance leads to the Processional Way, a wide avenue with walls decorated with bas reliefs on glazed bricks depicting lions which were hunted in the region.

At the heart of the ruins lie the two most famous parts, which I'm sure everyone has heard about. The first is the Hanging Gardens, one of the original wonders of the world. The Greeks nominated the Seven Wonders of the World. Six have been authenticated with one, the Great Pyramid of Giza, still standing. The exception is The Hanging Gardens, and it is even suggested by some experts that they never really existed. With due deference to the Greeks who knew a thing or two about classical buildings, I prefer to accept their existence.

They were built on the orders of King Nebuchadnezzar to please his Median Queen, Amytas, when she pined for the trees and plants of her native uplands. The gardens were built on different levels and thousands of trees and plants of many varieties were brought from all corners of the King's Empire. They were watered by an ingenious irrigation system. A series of rams, possibly operated by large metal screws, drew water to the top and it then filtered down to all levels. The well from which the water was taken was found in the original excavation, and can be seen today and still holds water.

Secondly, right in the heart of the site is the great sculpture called The Lion of Babylon. This is thought to have been a war trophy brought back to Babylon by one of the Babylonian kings.

Many things, which we now take for granted, emanated from the Babylonian times. The division of days into hours and minutes was calculated here. Using a base figure of 60 because it could be divided by so many whole numbers, the day was split into two 12 hour periods, and then into 60 minute hours making 24 a day.

The recording of information on clay tablets saw the development of the written word. Astrology was studied avidly since it was believed that the stars could provide a foretelling of the future and were the kingdoms of some of the Gods that they worshipped. Some of the 12 signs of the Zodiac are recorded here.

The well known saying, "The writing on the wall", predicting that something bad was going to happen has its origin in Babylon. King Belshazzar was now king some 23 years after the death of Nebuchadnezzar. He was holding a great feast in the Royal Palace when, as the story goes, a mysterious hand appeared, writing a message on the wall. The writing was in a language which none present could understand. The king sent for Daniel.

Daniel, as a boy, had been one of those captured by Nebuchadnezzar at Jerusalem and taken into exile with the rest. He was exceptionally able and intelligent and as he grew up, quickly became the spokesperson for the exiles and God's messenger or prophet. His ability was recognised first of all by Nebuchadnezzar who appointed him to be one of his chief advisers, much to the annoyance of Babylonian advisers who continually plotted against Daniel. They even got him thrown into a lion's den at one time, only for him to emerge unscathed, with his reputation greatly enhanced.

Daniel was kept on after Nebuchadnezzar's death. By now an old man, he obeyed King Belshazzar's command and went to the palace. When he saw the writing, he saw that it was written in Aramaic, the language of the Israelites. The words were "Mene, Mene, Tekel, Upharsin". Daniel recognised them as words relating to numbers, weight and division. He interpreted the message as a sign that the king's days were numbered, and later that evening the city was attacked and taken by King Cyrus of Persia.

Civilisation, as we know it, owes much to the Babylonians. It was a truly memorable experience and I felt very privileged to be there.

All too soon, my first visit to Iraq was over as Leon took me to the airport to catch the flight to Kuwait.

So what was I to make of it all? I was very impressed by the way the country was moving forward at such a pace. On arrival, I had seen large banners along the highway from the airport proclaiming the need to eliminate illiteracy. All week I had seen groups of schoolchildren in neat uniforms and I was told that mature students were being sent to Europe and America to study medicine, engineering, science and other skills which Iraq would need in abundance in order to maintain progress.

The Iraqi Dinar was a strong currency with 1Dinar being equal to £2. Presumably as a result of the revenue from oil, massive construction projects were under way, and Baghdad's skyline was a mass of cranes. More importantly, all the people seemed to have money to spend. The markets were always busy and my customers had difficulty in keeping up with demand for their products. I was aware that there was a lot more for me to do in the future.

One other thing surprised me, and that was seemingly open religious tolerance of faiths other than Islam. This certainly wasn't the case in Saudi Arabia or Kuwait. Although Islam is the religion of 95% of the population, there were Catholic and Othodox churches. There was even an Anglican church of St George, built in 1935 and dedicated in 1937. It was in the diocese of the Bishop of Jerusalem and Mesopotamia.

I also noticed great differences in people's appearances ranging from dark and swarthy to those who could have been mistaken for Europeans. I suppose it was as a result of Baghdad being on the crossroads of east/west trade routes for centuries and the intermixing of people caused by the regular conflicts.

In dress too there was great contrast between the traditional Arab wear and western clothing and that applied to women as well as men. Women seemed to have much greater freedom than say in Saudi Arabia, Kuwait or the Yemen, and were able to follow careers unthinkable in other Arab countries.

So there was much to be positive about. On the surface anyway there was no sign that the ruling Revolutionary Command Council, of which Saddam Hussein was effectively leader, had any hidden agenda. Admittedly it did have problems with neighbouring countries but this did not seem to deflect from the declared policy of a self-sufficiency programme for the domestic market, and the improvement of life for the ordinary people.

Bas relief, Babylon

Ishtar Gate Babylon

The Lion of Babylon

Hanging Gardens well, Babylon

Jumhuriya Bridge, Baghdad

Kadhimain Mosque, Baghdad

Scheherazade

Scheherazade & King Shahryar

Aladdin's Cave

The Magic Carpet

Morgiana statue, Baghdad

Juice seller, Baghdad

37

Folk Museum: café scene

Folk Museum: weaver at a loom

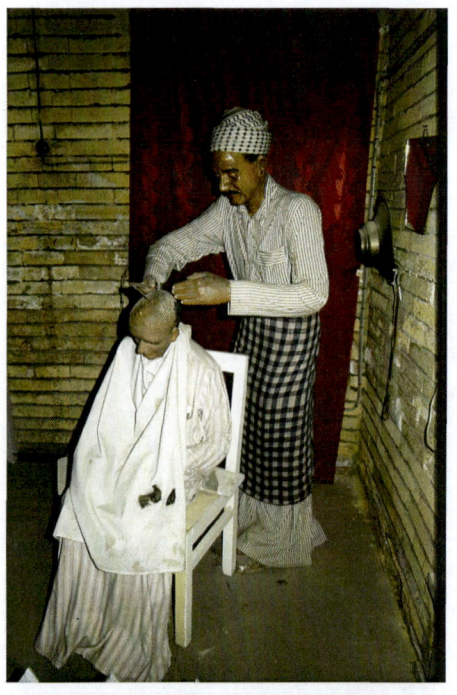

Folk Museum: the barber

Folk Museum: the tea maker

Ctesiphon

Liberty monument, Baghdad

Original Unknown Soldier monument

Original Unknown Soldier monument & 14th Ramadan Mosque

Newspaper vendor

Furniture maker – Baghdad

# 5

## EVERY MAN IS THE ARCHITECT OF HIS OWN FORTUNE. [trans from Latin]

Back in Bristol, there was much to be actioned, but with all the groundwork done, I returned to Baghdad 6 months later. There was a general air of unease about the place. Security at Baghdad Airport, and on the way into the city, was very noticeable and in the streets and main squares there was a most visible police presence.

Leon told me that it was all to do with the breakdown of relationships with Syria and the fear of terrorism. Our clients however were showing no signs of wanting to draw back from their projects and were still being encouraged by the authorities. Now that I had some idea of the layout of Baghdad, I used any spare time to wander around the streets and in particular the Shorja to see what goods were being sold, especially those relating to our packaging. Biscuits and sweets wrapped in our material were on display and I saw other packaging which had been printed locally and left a lot to be desired. I would buy packs and Leon would then contact the manufacturer and arrange a meeting. It was a very quick way of expanding our customer base.

The need for foreign assistance was still a priority and many countries, particularly those from Eastern Europe, saw this as an opportunity to benefit. As a result, delegations from all over the place were arriving on a regular basis. The numbers in these delegations varied from just a few to a whole plane load. The latter applied to some of the African visitors. All had to be accommodated and when the official hotel was full, the hotels in Saddoun Street were requisitioned regardless of their current occupants.

Pressure on hotel space was great at the best of times without this and on my second day, the hotel I was staying in was taken over. I had been to Samarra and on my return in the evening, longing for a wash or shower, found my things dumped in the corridor outside the room. I spent the night on a chair in the hotel lobby. Next day Leon managed to get me a room in another hotel further down Saddoun Street, but only after giving quite a few dinars to the manager.

I was now getting a very positive response on this visit. The Bunnia effect was convincing other companies to do business with us. Mr Al Bunnia was well respected and was, or rather *is*, a remarkable businessman. His grasp of what was going on in the development of all the company's businesses was considerable but it seemed to me that he was not prepared to delegate too much to the other members of his family at this stage.

Negotiations were always long winded with him and of course with other potential clients I had the language barrier to overcome. Although the majority could speak reasonable English, when it came to negotiating, they preferred to speak to Leon who would then translate their counter offers. I developed a method of blinking to Leon to indicate what % I was willing to drop having inflated the price in the first place knowing that I would have to come down. It was all rather comical but somehow it worked and everyone was happy in the end.

I was picking up some Arabic phrases.
| | |
|---|---|
| A greeting | Assalaam Alikum |
| Good morning | Sabah Il Khair |
| Hello/Welcome | Marhaba |
| How are you? | Kaif Halak |
| God willing | Insha Allah [used frequently!] |
| Goodbye | Fi Aman Illah |
| Yes | Na'am |
| No | La |
| Please | Mid Fadlak |
| Thank you | Shukran |

I also needed to know a few words for when I took a taxi by myself. Right – Yemeen, Left – Shimal, Straight – Gubal.

My pronunciation always caused amusement but it was an ice-breaker, as was my surname 'Freeman', which caused hilarity at the immigration desk when the official would inevitably comment and read out an exaggerated "Freeeeman!"

Customers were pleased to see me, if somewhat surprised that I had come back again. Mr Shakir in Mr Al Bunnia's office was delighted with the English dictionary I had brought for him. Everyone however seemed only too aware of a changing situation. The English language Baghdad Observer carried all the details of the visiting delegations all being greeted by Vice President Saddam Hussein and not President Al Bakr. Iraq TV showed little else and rumours about the leadership abounded. I suppose it was only natural that, with a history of three coups in recent years, people would be nervous about the future.

This did not hamper our business and I left with many new orders and contacts. Despite the tight security throughout my stay I still had the strong impression of a country moving forward. There were plenty of goods in the market. The cafés were always full. The various construction projects were making progress.

Education for all was still a priority and free, as was all medical and hospital treatment. Big subsidies were being handed to farmers to increase production and so reduce the need to import.

Whether or not the rate of development in the private sector was causing some disquiet at the top I don't know, but when I went back later in 1976 customers were distinctly unhappy. Certain measures had been introduced to slow things down. Applications for import licences would only be issued every six months and all commission agents had to register with the department of trade.

Commission agents had sprung up all over the place in the last few years and appeared all over the Middle East following the boom in the area's economy. Many had a poor reputation. In our case we had instances of "agents" coming to European packaging exhibitions, collecting brochures and then returning to their areas, calling on potential clients, and claiming to represent our company. They caused us a good deal of problems. I was not sorry that this new regulation had come into place and of course we were only too happy to provide Leon with the necessary accreditation. Leon however was very nervous because the penalties for operating without official registration were draconian to say the least: imprisonment for operating in the private sector and the death penalty for approaching a State organisation. So on this visit, with approval of his application still pending, Leon made it clear that he would accompany me only as a friend and certainly would not come to Samarra with me to the State Drug Company.

As a result I went to the central taxi compound to hire a taxi to get me to Samarra and back. Leon had told me roughly what the fare would be so I was ready to haggle until I got what I wanted. There seemed to be one man in charge and he was attempting to organise the drivers without much success. I was soon surrounded by a group, who must have thought I was a soft touch. I shouted out Samarra and the figure Leon had told me. This prompted a fierce argument among the men. Then one of them grabbed my arm and said "OK" and led me to his rather battered red and white taxi. It had plastic covers on the seats and with the temperature hovering around the 30ºC mark I felt as if I was being cooked. Still he was a competent driver. He had his son with him, aged about 10.

After I had finished my business at the drug factory we stopped by the ancient minaret built by Caliph Al-Mutawakkil around 850AD. The taxi driver had promised his son that he could climb it, so I decided to as well. I was alright going up, clinging to the handrail on the left hand side. The view was marvellous from the small watchtower at the top overlooking the walls of the old mosque and a little further away, the golden roof of the shrine of Imam Ali al Hadi, which dates back to the 13th Century. The descent, for me at least, was distinctly uncomfortable. I was suddenly aware of the sheer drop on my left hand side and it was difficult keeping hold of the handrail because of other people coming up. I must have looked really doddery as I tiptoed down!

Trouble was brewing elsewhere. I had intended to go on to Mosul from Samarra but reports came through that there was fighting in the area with the Kurdish separatists and therefore it would not be wise to attempt the trip at this time.

My visit to the British Embassy was a real step back in time to the days of "grace and favour" residences occupied by His/Her Imperial Ambassadors of State. The Embassy complex was situated in the Karkh district on the banks of the Tigris opposite the main commercial area and the Shorja bazaar. The site was protected by high walls, one of which ran along the river bank. The entrance had large metal gates and a small side gate guarded by an Iraqi soldier. Showing him my passport was sufficient for him to let me in, and I started to walk up a long drive towards the main building. I passed a large grassy area where in earlier times cricket was sometimes played, that still carried some croquet hoops. Tennis courts and a large swimming pool (empty) indicated a more relaxed lifestyle in former days.

In the main lobby I was vetted by a British security man and then shown into the commercial section. It soon became clear during our discussions that their whole emphasis was in dealing with the public sector and that their knowledge of the private sector was minimal, a trend, which I had found in other Middle Eastern markets. What was also clear was that the British Government supported the present regime, and saw it as an ally in a very troubled region. The British Council were promoting various cultural themes and had arranged for Brian Clough's Nottingham Forest football team to play a match at the national stadium.

There was some pressure being put on our ambassador to move to a special diplomatic quarter in one of Baghdad's suburbs where all the other embassies were, but this was being stubbornly resisted because of the proximity to the commercial centre.

The history of the Embassy building dated back to 1875 when it was known as the Palace of Khadum Pasha, the brother in law of the last sultan of Turkey. When General Maude led British troops into Baghdad in 1917, they took over the buildings, and in 1922 they were officially purchased for the then huge cost of £164,640.

It became an official Embassy in 1932 when Iraq became an official member of the League of Nations. The ambassador's residence was destroyed by fire in 1958 and wasn't restored until 1970.

During this visit to Iraq, it was announced on TV and in the press that Saddam Hussein had been made a general in the army, further fuelling speculation over what was happening to the President Al Bakr. As mentioned earlier, Saddam Hussein was not an army man like the President, so the appointment was significant in that he now had the support of the army. This did not go unnoticed among the people I met. He had also brokered a treaty with Iran principally to agree on the waterway boundaries in the Shatt Al Arab delta, but as part of the agreement, Iran agreed to stop supporting the Iraqi Kurds and their struggle was quickly and bloodily ended.

The main "enemy" now was Syria, which had been at loggerheads with Iraq for many years over its damming of the Tigris restricting its flow and causing problems to Iraq's agricultural programme. Now the emphasis was on Syria's involvement in the Lebanon and its growing relationship with Egypt and the formation of an Arab United Republic with Egypt.

Iraq had moved troops to the Syrian border and on my visit to Samarra, I saw many tanks and armoured vehicles heading out of Baghdad. Reservists had been called up too, and this left several companies short of key workers.

The Baghdad Press called Syria "A traitor regime" and towards the end of my stay, a curfew was imposed during the hours of darkness. One evening there was a total blackout lasting half an hour and some aerial activity could be heard.

It was a confusing picture as I left. On one hand business was continuing to grow steadily and there was no slowing down in the infrastructure programme. On the other hand there was undoubted tension regarding the president's position and the general uncertainty in the Middle East.

During two further visits in 1977, the tension between Iraq and Syria had grown significantly. In December '76, there had been an explosion at Baghdad Airport killing three people. This was stated to be an act of Syrian terrorism. Likewise, riots in Kerbala were blamed on Syrian pilgrims visiting a holy shrine in the city, although the more likely explanation was that it was a local dispute between Sunni and Shia Moslems.

Once again the Kurds in the north, even without Iranian backing, had attacked government troops forcing the army to withdraw from the Syrian border to concentrate on this matter.
Syria's occupation of Lebanon featured heavily on Iraqi TV and in the press. It was totally condemned, as was the assassination of Kamal Jumblatt also blamed on Syria.

Relations with Jordan were not great either and, as a result, supplies of fresh vegetables, eggs and dairy products were in short supply, with local production unable to meet demand.

Despite these problems, overall the economy was slowly improving. A major oil pipeline had been opened through Turkey, and with oil prices starting to increase, Iraq was getting the benefit.

The regional tension however had a knock on effect with our clients. There was a shortage of flour and sugar affecting their production but in contrast, shops were full of imported clothes, canned beer, spirits, photographic equipment, cosmetics and toys.

The major powers were now taking an active interest in the region and following the assassination of the Syrian Foreign Minister on a visit to Abu Dhabi, a high level delegation from Russia arrived which locked down Baghdad for almost a day.

Infrastructure projects were still proceeding apace. Most were being done by overseas companies. For instance, much of the road and bridge building was being done by Japanese companies, whilst new hotels were being built by Eastern Eupopeans. New hotels in Saadoun Street certainly relieved the accommodation problem for a short time anyway. Some even had telex facilities which helped me a lot.

My contacts were still growing and a week was no longer enough for what I wanted to do. One scenario which I had not reckoned on was that all the people I was meeting in the private sector actually owned their company and assumed that I was the owner of the packaging company. As a "humble" sales representative, this gave me some headaches as customers expected immediate decisions and were unimpressed if I continually referred back to base. My job was to "tailor make" the specification of the most suitable material and print quality needed for their product and as each job was different, it required careful costings. I kept a file of a range of options and could calculate an offer from these but it was a bit hit and miss. By and large I got away with it, but I did have to do some explaining when I got back to Bristol. The overall profit margins however were looking good which kept me out of "hot water".

Baghdad and Iraq in general were beginning to grow on me. I found the contrasts between the old and the new fascinating. A fleet of old Routemaster London buses had been acquired and plied the streets of Baghdad. Judging by the way they leaned over, they had severe suspension problems, and they were always crowded.

I decided one day to take the bus instead of a taxi. As I got on in Saadoun Street, I got some very strange looks. I handed the conductor 250 fils [50p] and he gave me 230 fils back! When we reached the terminus, all the other passengers waited and let me off first. When I told Leon about it later, he was a little shocked that I had done it and said that I should use only taxis.

Most offices closed around 1pm and reopened anytime after 4pm. If it wasn't too hot, I enjoyed wandering along the river bank, through the rose gardens or round the side streets just observing people's way of life. There were plenty of cafés where men sat outside reading the newspapers or playing chess or what looked like dominoes. The main streets had newspaper stands but no European publications. Small boys ran shoeshine stalls and barbers shops seemed always busy grooming Iraqi men, the majority of them had a moustache. Soft drink sellers carried large canisters on their backs. Small backstreet workshops were everywhere. Some were making furniture, or carrying out repairs to damaged cars with oxyacetylene equipment much in evidence. It all typified the industrious nature of the people.

Baghdad was an attractive place to work. The mixture of old and modern gave it character unlike the ultra modern Saudi Arabia or

Kuwait. I have already mentioned the river gardens and the Shorja. The mosques around the city were spectacular with wonderful mosaics and gold minarets. Included in these was the Al Bunnia family mosque, which had recently been completed. I was invited to go and see it and was very impressed by the décor. Only the finest building materials had been used most of which had been imported.

There were two major museums, which I wanted to see sometime. One was the folklore museum whilst the other was a museum of Iraqi culture but on this trip there wasn't time. I did manage to visit the folklore museum a year or so later and found the tableaux displays of the various aspects of Iraqi life very informative.

At the end of Saadoun Street was the monument to the Unknown Soldier. This was a graceful arch, simplistic but nevertheless very attractive. Sadly, later it was removed and replaced by a huge statue of Saddam Hussein, the one which the world saw being torn down when the American troops entered Baghdad in 2003.

The Monument of Liberty in the centre of Baghdad was also impressive. Other sculptures included one of Morgiana pouring the boiling oil into the barrels containing the 40 thieves. Also on the banks of the Tigris, a statue of Scheherazade, facing the King and keeping him entertained with her stories in order to spare her life.

Strictly speaking, I don't think Iraq can lay sole claim to Scheherazade as her origins go back to the days when Mesopotamia was part of a much wider region including modern day Iran [Persia]. Her name is undoubtedly Persian. The story goes that the Persian King Shahryar, was betrayed by his first wife, who he ordered to be executed. He was so embittered that even when marrying a new virgin, he had her executed straight away for fear of another betrayal. He was supposed to have had 3,000 girls killed by the time he was introduced to Scheherazade.

Scheherazade had studied the history of the region and was well versed in the folklore relating to all the various tribes. She could recite poems, sing songs and, as a daughter of a vizier, a court official, was well bred and had a pleasing personality.

As a virgin, she persuaded her father to let herself be offered as the king's next wife. On the wedding night, knowing the fate which beckoned, she asked the king if she could tell one last story to her sister, Dinazade. The king agreed and listened in. Amazed by what he had heard, he asked for another story but Scheherazade told him that as dawn was now breaking, he would have to wait until the next evening and she promised an even more exciting story.

So the legend of "One Thousand and One Nights" came into being with many stories that survive in one form or another to the present day.

The adventures of Sinbad the Sailor must have occupied many story telling sessions. How, during his seven voyages, he encountered many monsters, discovered new and dangerous lands, found treasure and survived shipwrecks.

Ali Baba's story is quite gruesome in parts. He had seen a band of 40 thieves stashing their ill-gotten gains in a woodland cave and had overheard the magic words needed to open the entrance – "open sesame". Once the thieves had gone Ali Baba entered the cave and took some of the treasure. He had been a poor man before, but now he was rich. His greedy brother Cassim finds out about the cave and goes to help himself to the remaining treasure, but forgets the password to get out and is trapped. The thieves return and kill him, and realise that more of their treasure is missing and resolve to track down the culprit.

There are many narrow escapes for Ali Baba and he is helped by a clever servant girl, Morgiana, who thwarts several attempts by the thieves. Finally however the thieves find out where Ali Baba lives and all but their leader hide in some large jars next to the house and plan to attack under cover of darkness. Morgiana discovers this and pours boiling oil into the jars, killing the thieves and when their leader arrives he finds them all dead and flees.

Swearing revenge, the leader bides his time and pretends to be a rich merchant. He gets invited to Ali Baba's house for dinner during which he plans to kill Ali Baba. He reckons without Morgiana however, who recognises him. As part of the after dinner entertainment, she performs a traditional dance, swirling around the room. When she is opposite the thieves' leader, she plunges a dagger into the man's heart, instantly killing him. Ali Baba is horrified but is filled with gratitude when he finds out the truth. He gives Morgiana her freedom and marries her.

Although these two stories have on occasions been adapted for pantomimes, the story most often appearing is that of Aladdin and his magic lamp.

A story of a poor young Middle Eastern man who somehow finds himself in a Chinese city. He is employed by an Egyptian sorcerer to get a magic lamp from a cave and he is given a special ring to help him in the task. The sorcerer double-crosses him and he is trapped in the cave. Rubbing his hands together, he unknowingly rubs the ring and a genie appears and helps him escape. He takes the lamp home to his mother, and as it is rather dirty, she decides to polish it whereupon another genie appears and says he will do anything that he is asked to do. Aladdin becomes rich, marries the emperor's daughter, and now lives in a magnificent palace.

The sorcerer, determined to get hold of the lamp, tricks Aladdin's wife into parting with it in return for a shiny new one. She had not known the magic power of the old one. The sorcerer orders the lamp genie to take Aladdin's palace and his wife to his Egyptian lair. Fortunately, Aladdin still has the ring and summons the first genie who transports him on a magic carpet to defeat the sorcerer and reclaim his wife, lamp and palace.

With stories like these, it is little wonder that the king kept Scheherazade alive. Each night she stopped telling the story at an exciting point and the king found he could not wait until the next chapter the following evening.

Of course the king came to realise how special Scheherazade was and she became a great queen. She bore him three sons and he became a much wiser ruler as a result of her influence.

All the stories have become immortalised in children's books, films, pantomimes and music.

Music too was also important to Iraqis. I wasn't too keen on the vocals but much of the instrumental music was very rhythmic and I was fascinated by one instrument called al qanoun and the skill needed to play it. This was done by running thumbs and forefingers, to which metal strikers were attached, over the instrument's 78 strings.

Early in 1978 relations with Syria got even worse and the borders with Iraq were sealed. This caused importers considerable problems because most goods came into the country from the Eastern Mediterranean ports in Syria. Many containers were trapped in Lattakia. Alternative routes were not attractive and were of course dearer. Aqaba in Jordan meant a longer sea journey and Basrah could not take container vessels. A container port at Umm Qasr had been started but was not ready to operate. Turkish ports did not have a good reputation.

Despite all this frustration, Iraqi companies were determined to push ahead and soon several major European transport companies opened up routes by road with vehicles large enough to take 20 tons. The route was through Turkey and in the winter months was extremely tricky and downright dangerous. We heard stories of many accidents and attacks by bandits but somehow the goods got through.

We were also hit by another problem. The Damascus Declaration decreed that any company supplying goods to Israel would be subject to a boycott in all Arab territories. We were careful, but another company in the group, which made tiles, had supplied an order to Israel, which was spotted and we were issued with a boycott notice banning exports from the UK. The company's lawyers submitted an appeal but we knew this would take time to be heard. Fortunately we had companies in Holland and France so we simply shipped goods to them and they invoiced from there. The boycott lasted about 12 months when it was agreed that our packaging had nothing to do with the other company's products.

Leon's tape business was doing well and he was getting a good commission return from our efforts too. With the Iraqi government still supporting a programme of self-sufficiency, Leon and his partner decided to apply to build a factory to coat paper and film and their proposal was accepted. A site was chosen and work was already under way. I went to see the project and the foundations had already been laid. I was intrigued by the site caretaker. He was living in a "dwelling" made out of empty cooking oil cans, with planks of wood over the top covered by a tarpaulin. His wife was there also and she had just cooked some of the Arab flat bread in a makeshift clay oven. We were given a piece each and it tasted very good!

Watching how other people live has always fascinated me. One day, I saw a taxi pull up, and the driver and passenger got out and went round to the back of the car. They carefully and very slowly opened the boot about 12 inches. The passenger put his hands in and pulled out two chickens, which he took into his house. He repeated this twice more and then fully opened the lid. The final chicken had got itself stuck behind the spare wheel, and defied all attempts to get it out. The driver then climbed into the boot and prodded it until it made its break for freedom, but the passenger managed to foil the attempt.

Thursday afternoons and evenings were also entertaining. This was the start of the Arab weekend and the time when weddings took place. Cars, lorries and pickups were used to transport wedding guests to the various hotels in central Baghdad where receptions would be taking place. Lorries would carry musicians playing loudly above the noise of the lorry's horn, and pickups could often be seen carrying wedding cakes with up to 19 tiers guarded on either side by men ensuring it did not topple over. Hotel managers frequently had major problems when the guests wanted to accompany the bride and bridegroom to the honeymoon suite and a near riot would take place when they were prevented from doing so. It appeared that many of the weddings were between people who lived outside Baghdad, and relatives wanted to make sure the marriage was consummated!

I was invited to a customer's home one evening for a meal. The man was in his mid 30s and had taken over a sweet factory from his father. Leon did not come with me, as protocol would have demanded that the man's wife would have had to dress all in black and stay out of the room because Leon was Christian. The rule did not apply where foreigners were concerned.

The meal, as I had come to expect, was **big** with plates piled with rice, lamb, fish, chicken and salads. I avoided the radishes, which were the size of tomatoes. They would have made me burp for a month!

Fortunately the man's English was good so conversation was not a problem. He was crazy about football and for the whole evening a tape was playing on the TV showing Sunderland v Liverpool and then Aston Villa v Manchester United.

He had one eye on the set all evening and every time a goal was scored he would leap up and down shouting. All good fun.

1978 was proving to be a good year for business. I now had over 30 customers most of whom had got used to seeing me turn up every six months, and treated me more like a friend than a supplier. Such was their desire to get product into the market that they sometimes forgot to train personnel in good hygiene habits. I was horrified one day when in a biscuit factory to see the operative sweeping the floor by the ovens and tipping the contents of the dustpan into the flour hopper. After that I made sure that on any visit to a factory I acted as quality inspector because our material was sensitive to moisture and if not wrapped properly after use could quickly become blocked and unusable. The trouble was that taking on this role was time consuming and with additional contacts every visit I was beginning to think that I would need three or four visits a year to run things successfully.

I was also concerned that some of the packaging machinery, which had been installed in 1974/5, was now in need of maintenance. From my experience I knew that the firms who had supplied the equipment were not interested in maintenance contracts and with the licensing regulations, it would have been difficult for Iraqi companies to get finance. They relied on local "engineers," who had no experience and it seemed to me that their solution to any problem was to turn the temperature up. This caused problems with seal strengths and the packaging always got the blame.

To counter any complaints, I persuaded the company to let me take with me, for part of the trip anyway, one of our technical representatives who regularly monitored UK companies' equipment. He corrected many malpractices and his advice and technical expertise was greatly appreciated by our customers and further strengthened our position in the market.

Leon's tape factory was completed, and he invited me to the opening ceremony. It required the traditional practice of killing a goat at the entrance, which didn't appeal to me at all. Leon, quite rightly, was very preoccupied with the factory, which left me on my own to meet with customers. This wasn't a problem as I knew my way round Baghdad now and all spoke English well.
Also they were getting used to seeing me on a regular basis and I felt that they now trusted me.

One morning Leon collected me from the hotel but we had not travelled more than a few hundred yards when his car came to a halt and he realised he had run out of petrol, which got him into quite a state. He flagged down a passing taxi and paid the driver to go and get some fuel. When we finally got to the factory, two lorries had arrived carrying large rolls of paper. Needing some labourers to unload the lorries, Leon asked one of his men to go and find some help. This he did but before they would start work he had to negotiate how much they would be paid. This involved a fierce argument, which lasted half an hour with much shouting and arm waving before a deal was struck. I noticed that in the cab of one of the lorries, there was a live chicken. I had seen some peculiar mascots in lorries in my time, but this was the oddest. Leon said that the driver had probably bought it in one of the villages as he was passing through so that if he got stuck anywhere he had a ready meal!!

On my last trip of 1978, I was accompanied by one of our company directors. With Iraq business now assuming some importance in our company's sales programme, I think he wanted to see how this new market worked. I met up with him in Kuwait and we took an early evening flight to Baghdad. On arrival we proceeded eventually through immigration and customs only to find a huge crush of people in the arrivals hall. Nobody was being allowed to leave the area. We heard that the King of Jordan was making an unscheduled visit and that all roads from the airport had been closed. We were kept there for the best part of five hours, and it was approaching midnight before we got outside. I knew that Leon would not have been able to come and meet us, so we found a taxi and I gave him the name of our hotel. I had an uneasy feeling that there might now be a problem in view of my past experience with visiting foreign delegations. My foreboding proved correct for when we got to the hotel we found that it had indeed been taken over.

The taxi driver offered to find us another hotel and we drove round and round the streets of Baghdad, but all hotels were full. Finally at 2.00am he found a small place down a back street, which had a couple of rooms. Frankly we were glad of anything but the "hotel" would not have appeared in any good guide! Breakfast in the morning consisted of bread and some rather strange jam. We declined the offer of eggs.

When I telephoned Leon, he told me that Baghdad was in lock down until the evening and that no one was allowed to travel about. So we had no choice but to sit it out until later. We could not help noticing however that during the day a steady stream of men came into the building with girls and disappeared into a back room. There was no doubt we were staying in a "house of ill repute"!!

Leon came and collected us that evening and managed to get us back to our original hotel as the Jordanian delegation had left. It was a rude introduction to Iraq for my director. Visits to customers were somewhat embarrassing. Having been introduced, customers then totally ignored him and spoke only to me. One even insisted on me going back to see him by myself. Still he was very supportive of what I was doing and it helped greatly when I returned to the office.

I had still not been able to get to Mosul but was determined to do so in 1979. What a year that turned out to be.

# 6

## ABSOLUTE POWER CORRUPTS ABSOLUTELY
ACTON

I had some shocking news just three weeks after I got back from my November 78 trip. A letter from one of Leon's sons informed me that Leon had been arrested and was now in the Abu Ghraib prison. Apparently the consignment of paper rolls which had arrived at the factory during my visit had been described on the documentation by the Swedish suppliers as gummed paper whereas the rolls were ungummed. To me this seemed just an honest mistake by the supplier. Customs had picked up the difference during their inspection and poor Leon was charged because the goods did not match the description on the import licence. There being no difference then between civil and criminal law, Leon was sentenced to 12 months in prison and fined ID2000, which was about £4000.

To make matters worse, his partner in the tape business was killed in a traffic accident. The man's widow had got involved in the business and was causing all sorts of problems.

Early in 1979, I was contacted by the London office of an Iraqi company acting for a new biscuit factory about to be opened in Iraq. During our meeting I explained our difficulty regarding our agency. This company told me that they had a contact in Baghdad who was looking to expand his agency business and also had a contact in Mosul. I agreed to meet the two on my next visit in March.

I discovered that Iraq Airways was running a daily service from Baghdad to Mosul. I was coming from Kuwait at a time when immigration and customs was normally quiet. I was due to land at 10.00am and connect with the flight at 11.00am. A slightly late arrival didn't help and by the time I had cleared entry formalities, the Mosul flight had closed. However a very helpful Iraqi Airways member of staff drove me out to the runway and with the luggage hold already closed, allowed me onto the Boeing 737 with my case.

It was only a half hour flight, and on arrival I took a taxi to the hotel which I had booked. It was a new one, but on getting there, I was informed that all reservations had been cancelled by the government, so I asked the taxi driver to find me an alternative. Eventually I checked in at a very rundown establishment thinking I only had to put up with it for two nights before going to Baghdad. When I enquired about an evening meal, I was told they could offer "meat" or "fish". My room had no hot water and the state of the bed linen made me sleep in a chair!

I can't say I was particularly surprised by the state of the "hotel". In my travels around the Middle East I had stayed in some plus 5 star establishments and others which would not rate even minus 5 stars. At least the hotels in Baghdad were somewhere in the middle. From the Ali Baba Hotel in Baghdad I wrote home "There is the usual mix up over the room. I have to spend a couple of nights in a small ante room just large enough for a single bed and a wash basin". Written next day "I was supposed to be getting a proper room today but when the porter came into the room I'd been given, there was a large lizard on the wall. It shot up on top of the curtain and then evaded all attempts to catch it. It then went to ground somewhere in the room so I had to go back to my "cell" for another night whilst they are dismantling the room trying to find it. It's midnight now and I can still hear them banging about upstairs".

Next day "I have been given another room now and I appear to be the only occupant! Apparently they did find the intruder in the early hours and disposed of it."

From the Ashur Banipal Hotel I wrote "It's not bad, and at least the fan works but the loo doesn't and it nifs a bit! There are the usual inhabitants, little yellow ones which are the fastest things over two yards I've yet seen. I can't grumble really. As hotels go here, it's pretty high up on the list and accommodation is so hard to get, you just have to be thankful you have a room at all."

From the Andalus Palace I wrote "This hotel is very nice. It's only been open a couple of months so the bugs haven't found their way in yet. There's nothing to swat and the toilet works, so life is quite dull. Mind you, there is no plug in the wash basin and every time I turn the tap on, water pours out of the pedestal base so I can shave and wash my feet at the same time."

Mosul is situated on the right bank of the Tigris, some 250 miles north-west of Baghdad, with a population of around 1,800,000. On the other side of the river lay the ruins of the ancient city of Nineveh.

Its name is Arabic meaning "The linking point" although another Arabic name for the City is Um Al – Rabi'ain meaning "Mother of two springs". It is perhaps an indication of the fertile nature of the area that it was given other names such as "The Paradise", "The Green" and "The Pearl of the North". Capital of the Nineveh Governorate, Mosul is Iraq's third largest city. Muslin, the cotton fabric, originated here centuries ago. It has an even more diverse mix of cultural backgrounds than Baghdad, with a history going back over 8,000 years. The population is made up of Arabs, Kurds, Armenians, Assyrians and Turks. Mosul has the highest proportion of Christians with churches dating back to the 13th century. The mosques too date back to the arrival of Islam and one in particular, the Great Nurid Mosque built in 1172AD, is famous for its strangely bent minaret. It is 52 metres high and can be seen from many parts of the city.

I looked forward to discovering more about the history of the area, but not on this visit as I had a lot to cram in two days.

Two companies were making high quality confectionery and I found a further two planning a similar venture, so it was clear to me that Mosul would have to be included on future visits. I met Khalid, the contact I had been given in London. I liked him immediately and he had a good knowledge of the food industry in the region. I explained the position regarding Leon and said it would probably be later in the year before I could confirm an agency once it had become clear what Leon's plans were. Khalid understood this and accepted our position.

One of the companies in Mosul was owned by two brothers. One was an English teacher in a Mosul college and on the second evening I spent a very nice evening with them and left with a large box of very nice sweets. Mosul businessmen had a hard time in getting their projects going as everything had to be organised through Baghdad and all licences were processed there, which meant many long journeys for the applicants.

On arrival in Baghdad, I managed to contact my customers and arranged various meetings.

I was contacted by Avo, one of Leon's sons, who told me that Leon would not be released until August, having served two thirds of the sentence. The family were terribly worried about his state of health because he had been suffering from a heart condition. I knew he had intended to come to London for an operation.

Avo told me that, once out of prison, his father intended to sell up and get out of Iraq. Now in his late 60s, needing medical attention, and with his business being managed by his late partner's wife, it was all too much. Quite how he intended to do it, Avo was unclear or wasn't saying, and I did not press the matter.

If this was going to happen, I realised that sooner or later I would have find someone else to represent us in Iraq, but I wasn't going to do this whilst Leon was still in prison. It would be too much like kicking a man when he was down. Avo proved a big help in ferrying me around Baghdad, but I was limited in what I could achieve.

Avo's news convinced me that I should be practical and make contact with the second businessman recommended to me by the London company. Moustafa was about my age, a very energetic type of man. He evidently had an office right in the heart of the commercial area, so was ideally placed. My only reservation was that his main business was in textiles and he had no experience of the food industry. His enthusiasm however was quite infectious and I agreed that once Leon's future was sorted, I would confirm the agency.

However there was a bigger international picture to be considered.

Middle East politics are complex at the best of times and 1979 produced a series of scenarios that could not have been predicted. First Egypt, having resigned from the Arab League, recognised Israel as a sovereign state. This led to the short lived union with Syria being dissolved, and sworn friends became sworn enemies. Likewise, Syria and Iraq, united in their condemnation of Egypt's action now became allies rather than enemies. President Al Bakr was instrumental in proposing a union between Iraq and Syria and the merging of the two socialist Baath parties. History shows that although this proposal gained popular support, there was one person to whom this idea was seen as a personal threat. That of course was Saddam Hussein. Such a merger would have pushed him down the "power" list to number three or four. Negotiations on the deal however did not go smoothly, with each side seeking to gain an advantage and be seen as the main player.

Saddam Hussein already had control of many parts of the government, but an event outside Iraq played straight into his hands.

During February 1979, the Shah of Persia was ousted following the return of the Ayatollah Khomeini and a huge Islamic state of Iran was created. Khomeini had for a time lived in exile in Iraq having been banished by the Shah. When Iraq and Iran signed a treaty of co-operation in 1975, it had been Saddam Hussein who had led the Iraqi negotiating team. As a result, Ayatollah Khomeini had to leave Iraq and live in Paris. So now there was an old score to settle. Iraq had an extreme Islamic republic on its eastern borders and another case of friend turned foe.

Almost immediately, calls came from the Khomeini regime for the Shia population of Iraq to rise up against the Sunni led government and become an Islamic state like Iran.

A strong response from a strong leader was required and Saddam saw this as his opportunity. President Al Bakr was not seen in this light. Having been to see the King of Jordan, Saddam Hussein forced Al Bakr to take "honourable retirement". The President appeared on Iraq television to announce his "decision" to step down and confirmed Saddam Hussein as the next President of Iraq.

When released in August '79, Leon set about selling his share of the tape business at a very low price. Then, having sent the rest of the family to London, he sold the house and came to London himself. Somehow over the years, he had accumulated sufficient funds in the UK to buy or rent a property in Kensington. Quite soon after his arrival, he had a major heart operation. I visited him soon afterwards. He was very bitter about the treatment he had received in Baghdad, and felt very strongly that the overall situation in Iraq was going to deteriorate. Now of course he could speak freely. He didn't like the idea of retiring completely and talked about starting a tape business in Jordan. His long term ambition was to emigrate to the USA. After two years he did move to California with most of his family. Before he left, I took my wife and family to meet them all in London and we spent a very pleasant time with them.

I kept in touch with him right up to his death in 1991. His health had been a constant problem and he had several more heart operations. In his last letter to me dated 17th August 1990, he wrote "If the President disappears for one reason or another, blood will fill the streets". How true was that prophecy! Leon had been the best of friends to me and had taught me a lot about Iraq.

By the time I went back in October '79, President Saddam Hussein was firmly in control. A charm offensive was launched aimed at the Western European governments, and the previous good relations with the Eastern Bloc countries appeared to have come to an end. Now significant numbers of British and European businessmen descended on Baghdad trying to get a share of the many public sector projects which had been announced as a result of Iraq being chosen to host the Non-Aligned Countries Conference in 1982.

This was a major prestige coup for Saddam Hussein, now seen as the strong man of the Middle East political scene and the right man to stand up to Ayatollah Khomeini, widely regarded in the West as a mad cleric.

Work had already started on two major hotels in Saadoun Street, opposite the Unknown Soldier monument. The Sheraton and

Palestine Meridian were to be showcase hotels to house the visiting delegates, whilst another luxury hotel was being constructed near the proposed conference site, to house heads of state.

As well as these projects, a new airport was to be built and the road building programme intensified. All this activity meant that the existing hotel accommodation was under even greater pressure than usual, but I was lucky in that, having stayed in the Al Abbasi hotel several times, I was regarded as a "regular" and got a room without any problem.

I now finalised things with Moustafa and Khalid and provided the necessary documentation so that the agency position could be formalised. Our business was still booming. It appeared that a small pack of biscuits was now a pre-requisite in every child's lunchbox at school and there was also a huge demand for biscuits in the markets, so much so that suppliers had difficulty in keeping up with demand. Merchants from other parts of Iraq were also buying large quantities of biscuits and sweets, and whichever factory I went to, there always seemed to be a lorry there waiting to load.

Moustafa's office was right in the heart of the commercial district in Rashid Street and on the 5$^{th}$ floor, looked down on the busy street. To get to it, I would take a taxi to Jamhouriya Street by the Shorja and walk right through the market to Rashid Street. This was something I really enjoyed doing and never tired of it. The atmosphere, smells (good and bad), the hustle and bustle, stall holders shouting, porters carrying huge loads and also pack horses all added to the general mayhem.

Leading off the various alleyways were even narrower alleys where some businessmen had offices and where some people lived. One morning as I was walking through, a bucket of slops came flying through an open window missing me by inches. An old lady looked out and burst out laughing as she saw the look on my face.

Despite the outward signs showing that business was booming, all was not as it seemed. A massive propaganda campaign had been launched to promote Saddam Hussein and the Baath Party. Portraits of ex-President Al Bakr had disappeared and every office, hotel and public building only had a picture of Saddam Hussein. Poster pictures of him appeared on every street. There was also a campaign to persuade people to become Baath Party members. Indoctrination had started in primary schools and a youth organisation called "Leaders" had been formed with boys and girls wearing a blue combat style uniforms.

It was well known that there had been a massive purge of people accused of plotting against Saddam and in a so-called anti-corruption drive 20 director generals of the various nationalised industries had been dismissed. Four of them had been executed.

The private sector was not immune and several prominent businessmen had disappeared including the owner of the stationery store, which I had visited with Leon on my first visit to Baghdad.

All these happenings left my customers extremely jittery and reluctant to talk about anything other than business, fearful of saying something out of turn which may be overheard by one of their employees who could quite easily be an informer.

Moustafa was proving to be an excellent choice as our agent and because of the location of his office, many clients called in after going to the bank.

I managed to get an internal flight to Mosul. The airport doubled up as a military base and security was very tight. I linked up with Khalid and apart from the two clients I had already, we quickly signed up three more. I was told that 100% loans were being given to companies in the north but people still had to travel to Baghdad to finalise things.

All in all, business prospects in Iraq had never looked better, and I was now having to allow 10 to 15 days each visit.

However during the summer months, the exchange of verbal hostilities between Iran and Iraq got more and more bitter, with Khomeini once again urging Shia tribes in the south to rise up against Sunni Saddam. The result was a deployment of a large part of the Iraqi army to the south especially in the Shatt al Arab Delta region close to the Iranian border.

Khomeini's hard line towards pro Western Kuwait and the United Arab Emirates were sending shock waves through the diplomatic communities in the West, as he was calling for all countries to become Islamic republics with a complete rejection of all Western influences. Needless to say the USA, UK and the rest of Europe feared the worst regarding oil supplies. The Arab League sought to calm things down but to no avail.

I had a trip booked for October 1980 but events took over. It is not entirely clear who started what, but on the 22$^{nd}$ September Iraqi forces crossed the Karoun River and occupied Khorramshahr and Abadan with its oil terminals.

The West's reaction was to support Iraq. Whilst Iraq was superior in military hardware, Iran's army outnumbered Iraq's by at least 2-1. Iraq's airspace was closed so it looked as if my travels to Baghdad had come to an abrupt stop.

# 7

## "HUMOUR IS THE ONLY TEST OF GRAVITY"
GORGIAS IN ARISTOTLE

Throughout the Gulf Region it was possible to obtain British newspapers 24 hours after publication and so keep abreast of what was happening both at home and overseas. That said, there were several regional papers, which also gave good coverage to the various events in the Middle East. The Arab News, Arab Times and the Kuwaiti Times were just three such journals. Such was the fragile nature of the regional political scene that during the 15 years that I travelled in the area, there always seemed to be some crisis or other that dominated the news. Peaceful solutions were always sought but rarely found.

Arab cartoonists had a wonderful way of highlighting the precarious nature of negotiations and here are a few examples of their creative take on the news of those times not that things have changed that much in the last 20 years.

"The Irish should be thankful the British don't 'retaliate' Israeli style"

Ex 'Arab Times'

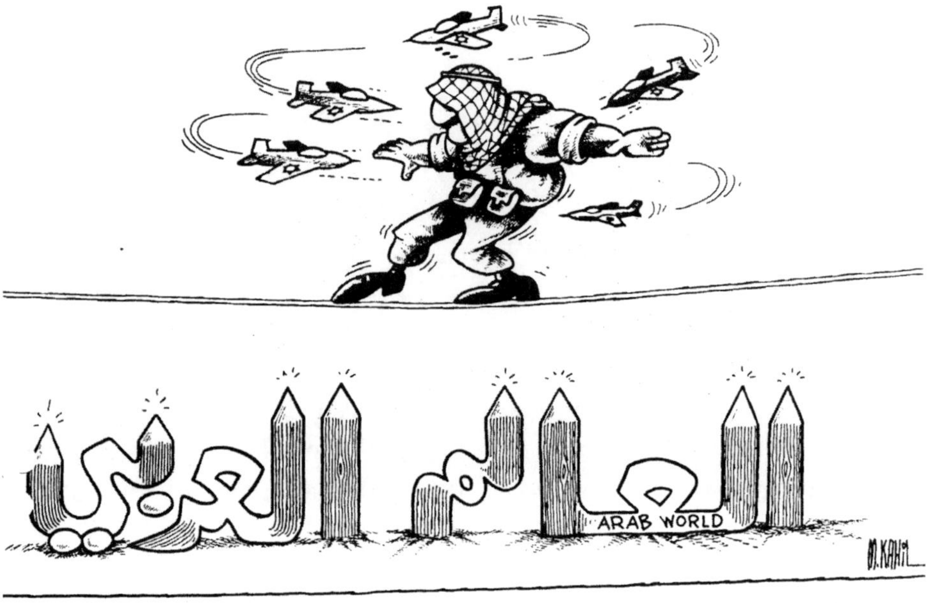
العالم العربي
ARAB WORLD
M.KAHIL

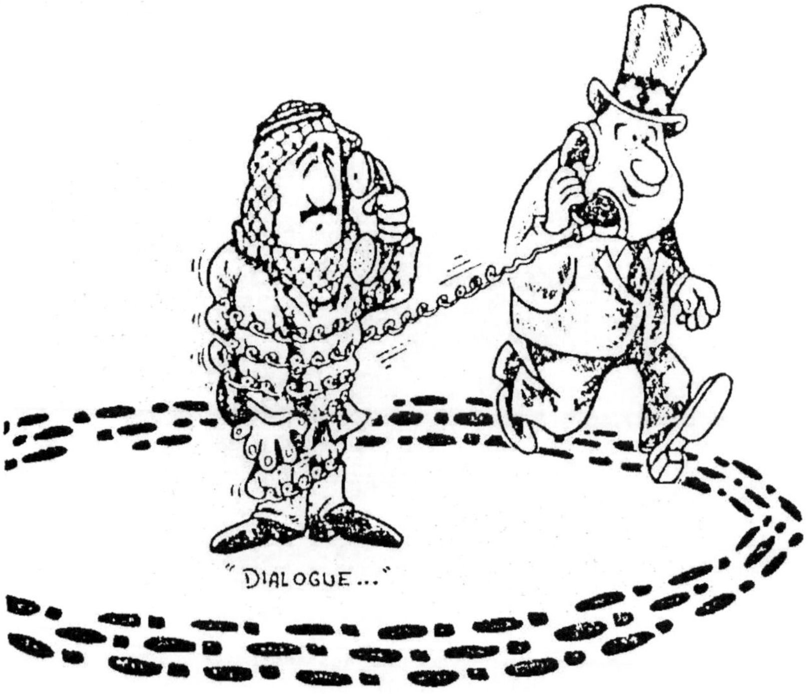
"DIALOGUE..."

arab news

M. KAHIL

*arab news*     SUNDAY, SEPTEMBER 13, 1987

# 8

## ALL ABOARD THE BAGHDAD BUS

With Iraq now off limits, I went to the Gulf States in November and found people there very nervous about what was happening to the north. Kuwaitis certainly feared that they would be invaded and many had left and moved their families and assets abroad.

When I got back to the UK around the middle of the month, I saw a report in The Telegraph that British Airways was running a bus to Baghdad from Amman. I used to use B.A. as a barometer on safety and I reckoned if they were operating the bus, then it was safe to go. I managed to get a quick visa and booked to go to Amman on the 3rd December and take the bus on the 4th. After the 6 hour flight to Amman, I was looking forward to a good night's sleep, but on arrival we were taken to a small minibus and told that we were leaving for Baghdad straight away.

The 600 mile journey started at 4.00pm and, after leaving the outskirts of Amman, we were soon on a long straight desert road. Our luggage was piled high on a roof rack. We were stopped regularly at military checkpoints all the way to the Iraqi border but there was still some way to go before we reached Rutbah where all immigration and customs procedures took place. Around midnight we stopped, and customs insisted that all of our luggage be unloaded, and taken into the hall for inspection. It was bitterly cold outside and not much better inside the buildings. It was 1½ hours before we were able to continue. Nobody was sleeping and I was only too aware that our driver was the only one on board and we were now on a narrow road with lots of heavy traffic coming the other way with blinding headlights.

As dawn broke, we were leaving the desert and approaching Ramadi, then just after 8.00am, we thankfully reached Baghdad. From the bus compound I took a taxi to the Al Abbasi, where, much to my relief, they had a room even though I had arrived a day early.

I called Moustafa to let him know that I had arrived and asked him to telex the office in Bristol so that they could let my wife know everything was fine. Then feeling absolutely exhausted I caught up on a few hours sleep.

Later that day, shaved, showered and refreshed, I met up with Moustafa and we tried to plan the next few days. There were many people to see and I also wanted to go to Mosul if time and conditions allowed. As recommended by the Foreign Office, I notified the British Embassy of my location in Baghdad. Customers were very surprised but pleased to see me. Needless to say the war was the main concern but people knew very little of what was going on and I was asked many times how things were being reported outside Iraq.

Iraq television, which was never a bundle of laughs at the best of times, was totally committed to putting out propaganda programmes showing the same action sequences time and time again. President Saddam was shown in military uniform visiting villages and encouraging the war effort.

There were many programmes of what I can only describe as military opera — all stirring stuff — plus a daily slot where the troops sent messages back to their families. Everything, in fact, except hard news.

The newspapers were no better and obviously subject to State control. Official bulletins were issued daily, as for example

"Statement No. 174 of the general command of Iraqi Armed Forces" but the language used fooled nobody. Iranian casualties were referred to as "aggressors killed", whilst, many Iranian tanks, guns etc had been "totally destroyed". On the other hand Iraqi armament was reported to be "out of order". The only real source of news was the BBC World Service, which was avidly listened to as and when reception was good enough.

The biggest effect that the war was having on the citizens of Baghdad had been, first of all, the blackout and then, in the last few days, electricity cuts of up to 10 hours a day. In Mosul and elsewhere, the cuts were lasting 23 hours a day.

The Iranian Air Force had managed to get one good strike at Iraq's main electricity power distribution plant at Nasiriya in the south, causing considerable damage. Since 80% of the country's power came from this source, the knock on effects were considerable. Fortunately most of our customers had generators to run their factories but many meetings took place by torchlight and being driven around Baghdad in the blackout was nerve-wracking to say the least. It was claimed that the plant would be fully operational within 7 days, but most people were sceptical.

Petrol rationing had been introduced to help the war effort. Cars with even numbers were allowed on the roads on one day and those with odd numbers the next. However it was generally thought that this was a ploy to cut down on the queues at petrol stations which could only operate when there was electricity.

As I had witnessed, the road from Jordan was a lifeline to Iraq with lorries bringing in supplies of all goods, especially foodstuffs. Shops were well stocked, except with biscuits and sweets, all of which were being sent to the armed forces. One of my customers was even making a special high nutritional biscuit for the army for which we supplied the wrapping material.

Baghdad supposedly had a good air defence system and had not suffered any damage unlike Mosul, which had become a soft target because it was not that far from the Iranian border.

With the support being given to Iraq by Jordan, Saudi Arabia and the Gulf States, there appeared to be no letting up in the country's expansion programme and if anything, it had intensified. Private industrialists were being given every encouragement and the capital loan ceiling had been raised from 60000ID to 200000ID or £400,000. Tenders for large public sector projects were still being published. Not all was going smoothly however. Several large projects, most notably the building of the Sheraton and Palestine Meridian hotels had ground to a halt because the contractors – Italian and Yugoslavian – had left because of the war. Other European contractors were now bidding to complete the work.

Whilst life in Baghdad continued as best it could given the power restrictions, people were understandably edgy. A couple of air raid warnings during my visit sent people rushing for nearest air raid shelters which had been constructed at key points. Both turned out to be false alarms. What was real however was the sight of cars returning from the south with roof racks carrying coffins draped in the Iraq flag, a stark reminder of the human cost of the war.

I did manage a trip to Mosul. I'm not sure where the information came from, but I learnt that a daily train was going to run. I went to Baghdad's main station and was able to book a berth on the overnight sleeper leaving at 8.30pm and arriving in Mosul at 6.30am. Ten hours seemed a long time when it only took 6 hours by road but with the fare only costing around £15 and a much safer journey, I was looking forward to it.

Iraq Railways had taken delivery of some new rolling stock from an Eastern Bloc source and the berths were extremely comfortable. There were quite a few military personnel on the train but I had a compartment to myself. I slept well and was woken by an attendant around 5.30am with some tea, bread and jam. Having washed and shaved, I was fully ready when the train pulled into Mosul exactly at 6.30am.

Railway buffs will tell me that this was the first stop on the east to west journey of the Orient Express. In better times the Express left Istanbul every Thursday and Sunday at 10.40am and arrived in Baghdad at 08.40am the next Sunday and Wednesday. Its route took it through Ankara – Aleppo – Ya'rubiya – Mosul. The return trip left on Mondays and Fridays.

Six-thirty in the morning was far too early for me to contact Khalid, so I made my way to the station waiting room. The layout was very plain, like something out of Kipling's India. There were seats, some with high backs shaped like coat hangers where, I guess, officers in the army would put their jackets. On the wall was a Smith's clock. It felt like a real time warp.

I had not been there but a few minutes when I was approached by an elderly man. He introduced himself in perfect English as the station master. He invited me into his office, and very soon tea appeared. He told me that he had been professor of English at the university in Sulemanieh. Now retired, he had taken this job, which was not too arduous as there was only the one train a day. The return train to Baghdad left at 8.30am.

I was curious about the station design, and he told me that it had indeed been copied from the plans of the stations built in India by the British and was constructed during the British occupation in the First World War. He was keen to practice his English, and we spent a very pleasant hour or so before Khalid came to find me.

Unfortunately, I was unable to get a return ticket as the train, 24 hours later was fully booked. Khalid took me on a rapid visit to our clients, all of whom were surprised to see me and, as in Baghdad, were keen to know what the news was. Mosul in the early days of the war had taken some punishment from the Iranian Air Force, but now Iraq had control more or less over its airspace and fighters were based at Mosul.

An early start by taxi got me back to Baghdad by midday 24 hours later. The rest of my time was taken up visiting as many clients as I could before I was due to leave on the 14th December. The British Airways office in Baghdad was still operating and I was told to report there at 3.30pm. There, with 32 other passengers, we boarded a coach. This looked far more promising than the minibus we had arrived in.

The atmosphere among the passengers was relaxed. We were a mixed bunch, mainly business people – British, French, German, Norwegian and several Iraqis including two women with small children. Christmas was only 12 days away, and no one was sorry to be leaving Baghdad.

It was still quite warm as we set off just after 4.00pm, going through central Baghdad and across the Jumhuriyah bridge over the Tigris, heading towards west Baghdad and then towards the desert road to Jordan.

All went well for the first couple of hours. We passed through several small towns and villages before crossing the Euphrates at Ramadi. As we entered the desert road, the sun was setting giving spectacular orange and red effects over the landscape.

It was then that the defects in the coach started to become apparent. It was Czech built and first of all we found that the coach heater was not working. I was sitting next to a water engineer from Gloucester. He had brought a bottle of whisky with him with the intention of drinking himself into a good night's sleep.
Of course with the alcohol thinning the blood, he was already feeling uncomfortable. With ill fitting windows and floor panels, the cold evening air was soon circulating around the coach, and as the evening turned to night time, the temperature fell to zero. Only two blankets could be found and these, quite rightly, were given to the two women with children.

Still, the coach driver was making good time, only five hours to Rutbah, which was half way. The prospect of getting to Amman in four hours less than it had taken us to reach Baghdad on the inward journey, helped us, to some extent, ignore the cold.

Our optimism was ill founded. Before reaching the Iraqi immigration and customs post we had to stop and refuel at the one and only petrol station in this small desert town. Normally coaches had priority, but the driver found his way blocked by at least 70 big lorries queuing for diesel fuel. Try as he might, he could not get anywhere near the pumps. For the best part of an hour he tried all sorts of manoeuvres without success. Finally in desperation he drove up the wrong side of the road, horn blaring, full headlights blazing, taking huge risks considering the heavy traffic coming towards him.

Having finally refuelled, we were driven to the immigration and customs compound. All our cases had to be unloaded and placed in a line by the side of the coach. We then had to identify our case and then take it into a hall for inspection and then take it back to the coach. Then, standing in line at dead of night, in the freezing cold, we waited for immigration to issue an exit stamp in our passports. By now, I couldn't feel my feet and my legs felt like lumps of lead. Everyone was in the same state. The only consolation was the night sky. In the total darkness the stars and constellations shone in a way I had never seen before or since.

We staggered back onto the coach and it ground on through the night but, before reaching the actual border between Iraq and Jordan, we were stopped several times by Iraqi checkpoints. At the border the Jordanians quickly checked the passports and did not bother with a customs inspection.

Once across the border we ran into thick fog, and our speed was reduced to a crawl. Many passengers were suffering with the cold and the man sitting next to me could not stop shaking. With the fog clearing, we sped, up passing a Jordanian armoured convoy. Dawn was breaking and we were approaching some hills some 10 miles from Amman. Suddenly the driver slowed right down. The reason – a couple of inches of snow which was making the road surface treacherous. We slowly made our way into Amman through flurries of sleet and just before 8.00am, tired, cold, hungry and thirsty, we crawled off the coach into the hotel that British Airways had booked for us. Imagine our consternation, therefore, when we discovered that the hotel was not expecting us until the next day and had no rooms available.

By this time we were all feeling pretty mutinous and the B.A. representative started ringing round trying to find a hotel to take us all. It took a while but he managed to get us into the Sheraton, so we loaded our cases once more onto the coach despite the driver's protests. He could see that we were in no mood to argue, so he grudgingly took us across the city to the Sheraton where, after checking in, we headed straight away for the coffee shop. There, unshaven and unwashed, I got through several cups of coffee and a plate of bacon and eggs. Food and drink had never tasted so good! Afterwards, a shave, a hot shower and several hours sleep restored me to the human race. The B.A. flight next day was on time and I was very glad to get back home.

# 9

## WAR IS DEATH'S FEAST – G. Herbert

By the time I went back to Baghdad in May 1981, British Airways had not resumed flights but was still operating the bus service from Amman. The British Embassy were still recommending this route and insisting on their own staff using it. Royal Jordanian and Iraqi Airways however were running a daily flight from Amman. Once on the bus was enough for me, so I opted for the air route.

The flight took off at 8.00pm and as soon as we left, all blinds were drawn and the cabin lights were dimmed. The aircraft did not appear to ascend to any great height and I was told later that flights flew at low level and were escorted in Iraqi airspace by fighter jets, and that the landing lights at Baghdad Airport were only switched on at the last minute. However two hours on the plane was infinitely better than 16 hours on a bus, even with the supposed added risk. Blackout restrictions made finding a taxi outside the airport difficult and the ride into central, blacked out, Baghdad was "adventurous" to say the least.

Early contact with Moustafa and customers showed they knew little of what was going on in the war. Instead of me asking them, they were asking me! All they were getting was the propaganda being churned out on TV and in the press. I was able to tell them from the reports on British TV and our newspapers, that fighting was taking place across the Iranian side of the Shatt al Arab delta around Dezful and Abadan.

A communiqué was issued every day by the Government. Typically it would announce that six times as many Iranian "aggressors" had been killed as Iraqi "martyrs". The fact that the authorities were now admitting casualties was seen as significant by the people I met and all thoughts of a quick war had vanished.

It was further announced that the family of Iraqi "martyrs" would receive 25,000 Dinars [approx £50,000] and some free land as compensation. I could not help noticing the increase in the number of private cars and taxis with roof racks carrying coffins draped in the Iraqi flag.

I also heard from several sources that parents whose sons were studying abroad were desperate for them not to come home after finishing their courses and were pleading with them to find reasons to stay where they were. I was given several contact numbers by anxious parents, for when I got back to the UK.

With apparent stalemate in the war, international spotlight had moved away and was now focussed on the rapidly deteriorating situation in Beirut and also the escalating hostilities between Israel and Syria.

In Baghdad blackout restrictions limited my visits to daylight times only. Frequent power cuts were making life uncomfortable as the temperature in May was reaching 30-35°C and with air conditioning units often not working, it was a sweaty time for me. However most factories seemed to be working as most had standby generators which came in very handy.

Getting to Mosul got harder again. Understandably there were no flights, and all train and coach services were reserved for military personnel only. So it was back to a taxi ride. The road building programme was still under way although it had slowed down due to a lack of skilled labour. The dual carriageway north now extended to two thirds of the 400km journey, just north of Tikrit, Saddam Hussein's birthplace. Thereon it was back to the narrow road with nose-to-tail heavy traffic in both directions, all travelling at great speed mainly to and from Turkey. Most lorries were grossly overloaded or inefficiently loaded and as usual the standard of driving verged on the lunatic! The results of this mayhem were clear for all to see as frequent wrecks and debris littered each side of the road. It seemed to have little effect.

Mosul itself had not had an air raid since the beginning of December. It had been in easy reach of the Iranian Air Force or at least what remained of it, but with its airbase now operative, attacks had ceased as had attacks on other northern cities such as Arbil, Kirkuk and Sulemanieh. These Kurdish areas had previously been seen as hostile, or at least unsympathetic, to the central Government of the Baath Party in Baghdad whose relentless central control always seemed to favour Baghdad and the Governorate it was in.

The war however had brought about some sort of national unity, and differences had been put aside. The Baath Party had forged strong links with the Ninevah Governorate, of which Mosul was the capital, and the region now provided one of the most respected regiments in the Iraq army.

President Saddam Hussein now recognised the support he was getting and started to pay a good deal of attention to the region. It started to receive more financial support for new projects to boost and broaden the area's economy. Provision for import licences however did not devolve to Mosul and businessmen still had to travel to and from Baghdad.

My business here was growing all the time and it was difficult to fit in all the visits in two days. This time I was able to get a room in the one reasonable hotel, which was just a few hundred yards from the site of Nineveh, once, the proud capital of the Assyrian Empire.

Its history dates back to around 700BC when it became the third capital that the Assyrians built after Assur and Nimrud. Both of these were some 10 to 20 miles south and the site of Ninevah was considered to have a more strategic position in the area. It was soon developed as a cultural, religious and administrative centre for the whole region.

The city walls were 12km in circumference and originally there were 15 gates into the city, each one named after an Assyrian God.

Excavation of the site was started in the early 1800s by the French consul, resident in Mosul, who was curious about huge mounds on the other side of the River Tigris. He employed local Arabs to dig and soon discovered the walls of a building, which was identified as having been the Palace of Sargun II. Many relics, sculptures and other artefacts were found most of which ended up in European museums.

These early excavations were followed up by a young British adventurer, Sir Austin Henry Lazard and on another part of the site, the lost Palace of Sennacherib was found. It had 71 rooms and huge bas-reliefs. He also discovered the Palace and Library of Ashurbanipal containing 22,000 Cuneiform inscribed stone tablets dating back to 626BC.

Further exploration towards the end of the 19th century unearthed the ruins of many more palaces with more artefacts and bas-reliefs reflecting the life of this civilisation. The bas-reliefs depicted both their peacetime and wartime life. They showed what ordinary buildings were like and what people wore. Kings were shown in all their finery. Again most of the things found were transported to European museums.

The 20th century showed no let up in expeditions to further explore the site. The British Museum funded a dig by Leonard William King, and also in 1927, by Campbell Thompson. After the end of the Second World War, in the late 40s, the Iraqi authorities themselves organised an excavation and alongside Iraqi archaeologists, a British Professor David Stronach led a team from the University of California.

From details of plans discovered, a reconstruction of the Mashki Gate was built and a small museum was opened where some artefacts could be viewed as well as a huge bas-relief of a winged bull.

The Nineveh site is so large that there are still wide areas to be explored and further secrets revealed. Hopefully, when this happens, anything found will be kept in Iraq.

There are frequent references to Assyria, Babylon and Nineveh in the Old Testament of the Bible, signifying their importance in those times. The first mention is in the Book of Genesis where it is recorded that Nimrud, a descendent of Noah's sons, went to Assyria and built three cities including Ninevah.

The Assyrian Empire features a lot in the Books of Kings and Chronicles and then in the Book of Jonah. Nineveh is described as a "city so large that it took three days to walk through it".

Jonah was the prophet who tried to disobey God's commands. Nineveh had acquired a reputation for wicked behaviour and Jonah was commanded by God to go there and reprimand its people. Instead of following instructions, Jonah headed in the opposite direction to the port of Joppa and booked a passage on a boat sailing to Spain. Once at sea, the vessel ran into a terrible storm with Jonah sound asleep below. He was woken up by the terrified captain and crew and asked to pray to his God to abate the storm. Jonah, realising that this was God's punishment for disobeying orders, told the crew to throw him overboard and that the storm would cease if they did. At first the captain refused and tried to make it to a sheltered harbour but the storm only intensified. Reluctantly, they agreed with Jonah's request and threw him into the sea and immediately the storm subsided. God had not finished with Jonah and the poor chap was then swallowed alive by a whale. Inside the whale, Jonah prayed for forgiveness and after three days we are told that the whale spat Jonah out onto a beach.

Jonah then travelled to Nineveh and warned the king and its citizens that if they did not mend their ways, the city would be destroyed in 40 days. The Bible story continues:-

"The people of Nineveh believed God's message. So they decided that everyone should fast, and all the people, from the greatest to the least, put on sackcloth to show that they had repented."

When the King of Nineveh heard about it, he got up from his throne, took off his robe, put on sackcloth, and sat down in ashes. He sent out a proclamation to the people of Nineveh: "This is an order from the king and his officials: No one is to eat anything; all persons, cattle and sheep are forbidden to eat or drink. All persons and animals must wear sackcloth. Everyone must pray earnestly to God and must give up his wicked behaviour and his evil actions. Perhaps God will change his mind; perhaps he will stop being angry, and we will not die."

God saw what they did; he saw that they had given up their wicked behaviour. So he changed his mind and did not punish them as he said he would."

Jonah had a massive sulk about this outcome and pleaded with God to let him die. So he went outside the city and built a shelter and the story goes that God let a tree grow up around the shelter to provide shade but it soon withered and Jonah had to suffer the heat of the day. Jonah said again "I am better off dead than alive" to which God replied "What right have you to be angry about this plant?" Jonah replied "I have every right to be angry, angry enough to die." but God said to him "This plant grew up in one night and disappeared the next; you didn't do anything for it, and you didn't make it grow – yet you feel sorry for it! How much more then, should I have pity on Nineveh, that great city. After all, it has more than 120,000 innocent children in it as well as many animals."

However the return to "righteous ways" in this Assyrian capital didn't last and in the 7$^{th}$ century BC, Nineveh was attacked and overrun. The Book of Nahum contains a graphic description:-

"The enemy soldiers carry red shields and wear uniforms of red. Their chariots flash like fire. Their horses prance. Chariots dash wildly through the streets rushing to and fro through the city squares. The attackers rush to the wall and set up the shield for the battering ram. The gates by the river burst open. The palace is filled with terror. Horsemen charge, swords flash, spears gleam! Corpses are piled high, dead bodies without number and men stumble over them."

So a great city and the Assyrian Empire came to a bloody end. As with my visit to Babylon, I felt a great sense of history. I walked up to the reconstructed gate with the bas-relief of the winged bull and was permitted to look around the small museum. No doubt in years to come Nineveh will reveal more secrets of the life and times of the Assyrian Empire.

# 10

## VANITY OF VANITIES – ALL IS VANITY
### ECCLESIASTES

Back in Baghdad, a massive publicity campaign was taking place to promote the image of the President, Saddam Hussein. I had noticed in Mosul a huge poster of him, all of 30 feet high. Photographs of the old President, Al Bakr, had now disappeared and even larger pictures of Saddam Hussein now decorated the walls of all offices, hotels and public buildings. Posters bearing his image appeared on nearly all streets. His hands had also been modelled. Hands giving the victory V sign, about 3 feet high, had been mounted on concrete pillars around Baghdad. Unfortunately many had been mounted the wrong way giving a rather rude result! Casts of his hands too, formed part of a ceremonial arch at the main military parade ground. The arch consisted of the hands holding a sword on either side, forming the arch.

A charm offensive had also been launched on the Christian minority, which represented 10% of the total population of Iraq. They were singled out for special attention and extra Government aid was being given to equip Christian schools and to refurbish churches of all denominations and monasteries which had fallen into disrepair.

Saddam Hussein, now promoted to a Field Marshal either by the army or more likely by himself, was still actively talking up the Non Aligned Conference due to take place in Baghdad in 1982.

Work on several major projects however had stalled. In particular, the building of the Sheraton and Palestine Meridian hotels had more or less come to a standstill when the Eastern European contractors did not return from leave, citing the war as the reason. To counter this, new contracts were awarded to French, West German, Finnish and UK contractors. The shortage of local labourers due to the ever widening age range for conscription meant that "guest" workers were now being recruited from as far away as Thailand and Bangladesh.

What with conscription and the dreadful casualty rate [not officially admitted] and the fact that a war which was only supposed to last a few weeks was now in its second year, a general weariness seemed to affect most people. Iraqi TV, trying to lighten the gloom, knowing the Iraqis love of football, showed the English Cup final between Tottenham Hotspur and Manchester City [3-2 to Spurs] and a few days later England v Brazil.

Among the people I met, I didn't find that this distraction made any difference to the worry they had about the possibility of their sons being called up for the army. Once more I was given contacts to get in touch with on my return to the UK.

It also appeared that the message had got through to Iraqi doctors training and working in Europe and the USA. A shortage in hospitals, due to conscription, was not being filled by returning qualified doctors, who, once qualified, were being offered more attractive posts in their host country. To tempt them back, they were being offered huge salaries, cars, houses and land. I don't think there were many takers.

Just as support for the regime brought tangible rewards, so apparent dereliction of duty brought equally swift results. An enquiry was held into the Nasriyah power plant bombing by Iranian jet fighters in December 1980, which resulted in crippling the country's electricity distribution system. The attack was unopposed and all the Iranian aircraft returned to base unscathed. Twenty-three people were tried and found guilty of inadequately protecting the station and were shot!

A sort of ethnic cleansing was also taking place. Anyone of Iranian descent was being arrested and deported. It affected one of my best customers. Two brothers ran a very successful confectionery company and had recently spent over £1 million in new equipment. Both were Iraq born and bred, but their grandparents were Iranian. They were arrested without warning at night and I was told they were bundled into the back of a truck and taken away presumably to the Iranian border. The company was put up for sale by the Government, which then pocketed the proceeds.

By the time I returned to Baghdad in November '81, Baghdad was looking more like a builder's backyard than the showpiece city that Saddam Hussein wanted to present to the outside world's media when it came to report on the Non Aligned Conference, now less than 12 months away.

Frantic efforts were being made to finish all the various projects. Far Eastern workers brought in earlier in the year had not provided the answer and most had returned home. Language difficulties were quoted as one of the reasons. Now, thousands of Egyptian workers were being flown in by the 747 load, and by the end of 1981, it was estimated that there were no fewer than 2½ million in Iraq. Despite their deep political differences Egypt was providing the labour, benefiting of course from funds being sent home by the workers. The expenditure on the war was biting deep into Iraq's financial reserves and help was secured from Saudi Arabia to underpin the Treasury.

As a result of this support, Saddam Hussein was able to throw more money at the projects and no expense was spared in bringing in technicians, engineers, construction workers and all types of skilled craftsmen from all corners of the Western world. This caused severe problems in providing accommodation and all hotels quickly became overbooked. Hotel reservations were not worth the paper they were written on, and once again, rooms were being shared by 2 or 3 occupants. In the hotel I was in, I shared a room [twin bedded!] with a Kuwaiti businessman. I was one of the lucky ones because in the basement 29 people were sleeping on mattresses.

Because of all the upheaval, getting around Baghdad was difficult as many roads were closed. A new sewerage system was under way and at the same time a new telephone exchange with all the relevant cabling was being installed ready for the 1982 conference. As a consequence long trenches had been dug along the roads and pavements.

Little hard news of the war was given except that Iraq was "winning". The conscription age was raised yet again and all males born between 1951 and 1954 were now being enlisted.

There was much evidence of troops and equipment being moved around. During a visit to a factory in Mahmoudiyah, a few miles south of Baghdad, I passed several convoys of tanks and trucks carrying troops.

Another journey to Mosul by taxi proved beneficial for our order book and for the taxi driver. With all buses and trains now reserved for the military, taxi drivers had doubled the fare! It's an ill wind!

It was reported that a big push was expected in the war zone before the winter rains set in. It was admitted that the Iraq Army had been forced back to the border and that Abadan was now back in Iranian control. Casualties on both sides had been massive. Everyone I spoke to was very depressed about the situation. The president's popularity was at an all time low. The posters on the streets carrying his picture, which had been such a feature when I visited earlier in the year, were now tatty and torn. The victory V hands had disappeared.

Despite the gloom about the war, the standard of living for ordinary Iraqis was being maintained. The commercial office at the British Embassy were predicting that Iraq's finances were in pretty poor shape and that Iraqi banks were requesting extended credit terms. Not such good news for me.

Even though Iraqi airspace was open during the hours of darkness, getting to and from Baghdad was proving to be problematical. Iraq Airways had four flights a day in and out of Europe and two from Amman. All were fully booked weeks in advance, and on return flights it was necessary to visit their office daily to make sure of a flight confirmation. Even then, judging by fierce arguments at the check in desks, this was no guarantee of a flight.

# 11

## TO THE WISEST OF MEN AN ERROR IS FATAL
ANCIENT ARAB SAYING

Nineteen-eighty-two was to be the year that the spotlight of the world fell on Iraq and Saddam Hussein in particular. He was to be host to the Heads of State and their delegations from all the non aligned countries of the world. But the problems regarding Iraq/Iran – Syria/Lebanon – Israel against the rest were occupying the minds of all at the United Nations.

In April, just five months away from the start of the conference, it seemed to me that there was no way that Baghdad was going to be ready in time. Not content with replacing the sewerage and telephone systems, the authorities had decided to refurbish the drainage in central Baghdad and most pavements had been closed and deep trenches dug.

With electricity supplies being constantly interrupted and 50% of the telephone system out of action because of the replacement work, businesses were finding it hard to cope. Trying to make appointments was a nightmare and we simply had to chance making contact with our clients.

The Egyptian workforce had now been joined by "guest workers" from Japan, Korea, Pakistan and the Philippines. They were being housed in vast encampments of wooden chalets dotted around the outskirts of Baghdad and were being bussed or taken by truck each day to their particular project. Their European bosses were of course based in those hotels still open and pressure on room occupancy continued but it was noticeable that there were fewer Europeans than before. Whether they had been frightened off because of the war or just got fed up with the hotel situation was hard to say. The Al Abbassi, where I was staying, had a fair proportion of British engineers and contractors. They took a liking to the local beer and on the Thursday evening [start of the weekend] treated Saddoun Street to a raucous version of *You'll Never Walk Alone* until silenced abruptly by the local police who obviously had no musical appreciation!

During a visit to the British Embassy, now a must for all British visitors to register where they were staying, I was told that in their opinion the Non Aligned Conference would not take place, which would be a huge embarrassment for Saddam Hussein.

Whilst at the Embassy, I was tipped off about an easy quick way to get to the commercial centre of Baghdad where Moustafa's office was. Finding a taxi outside the Embassy usually took ages and then it could take half an hour to get through dense traffic on the Ahrar Bridge before reaching Rashid Street, which, during daytime was always crowded with cars, lorries and people. Down on the river bank, behind the Embassy, a small boat was operating a ferry service across the Tigris, taking about five minutes. It landed passengers on the bank right next to the commercial area and a couple of minutes from Moustafa's office. The boat, about the size of a small rowing boat fitted with an outboard motor, was doing a steady trade and I didn't have to wait long. I paid the man 250 fils, about 50p, but I suspected that the locals paid far less. The only snag was that there was no landing stage and I had to step out on to a muddy bank before reaching the pavement. No problem though as there were always plenty of shoeshine boys ready to clean shoes for a few fils, and this was a good pitch.

It was hard to believe there was a war going on. According to the TV news bulletins, which were broadcast in English for 15 minutes each day, and in the English language Baghdad Observer, Iraq was still winning the war and the casualties were 10-1 in Iraq's favour. However it was noticeable that words like "settlement", "compromise" and "peaceful solution" were now appearing in print, and much prominence was given to the efforts of an Islamic Peace Mission which had recently been in Baghdad.

On Thursdays and Fridays, many soldiers could be seen on the streets and in the cafés, having returned from the front on a 48 hour pass. There were now no blackout restrictions and cars no longer had to paint the headlamps blue.

It was when I spoke to individuals that it became apparent how much the war was affecting their lives. Everyone seemed to have a close relative who had been killed, wounded or taken prisoner. Several times meetings were cancelled because my client had to go to a funeral. People were depressed and longed for peace but feared it would be a long time coming. Estimates now put the number of men in the army at 500,000.

The Non Aligned Conference was now less than 6 months away and it was hoped that there would be a resolution to the conflict before then. I didn't tell them what the British Embassy's opinion was on that score.

Saddam Hussein's popularity had fallen even further. Very few posters remained in the streets and those that were left were faded and torn. No one had gone so far as to take down the obligatory pictures in the offices, shops and hotels. Shops still displayed watches, key rings, wallets and other items bearing his portrait.

Some good news was that the two skyscraper hotels, the Ishtar Sheraton and the Palestine Meridian were now nearing completion. In fact the Meridian already had four floors open for business.

The bad news was that an austerity programme had been announced and no new public tenders were being issued and the private sector faced cuts of up to 60% in their licence allocations.
Food producers however were quickly assured that they would receive special treatment and some were being asked to get involved with some of the State owned industries such as flour, sugar and poultry/egg production, all of which were badly under-performing.

I was making contact with more companies outside of Baghdad and Mosul. One new company was in the small town of Musayib some 35 miles south of Baghdad. The factory had been built alongside the river Euphrates and consisted of a number of breeze block buildings with metal roofs. A few cooling fans made no difference to the temperature and I felt that an oven for cooking the biscuits was hardly necessary! Nevertheless production was going ahead and we had a new customer. He told me that he planned to move to a better site in the Mosul area some time in the future.

A further 35 miles to the south was Kerbala, a city very important to Iraq's Shia Moslems. As capital of the Kerbala Province, it had a population of over 500,000 and is considered by all Shia Moslems to be one of their holiest cities after Mecca, Medina, Jerusalem and Najaf.

The city is built round the tomb of Masjid al Hussein their chief saint and grandson of the Prophet Mohammed. It is a place of continual pilgrimage and the gold domed tomb with its three tall minarets, dominates the city.

For Shia Moslems, it is a centre of religious instruction and throughout the city there are over a hundred mosques as well as 23 religious schools, which probably explained the large number of Mullahs I saw in the streets.

In history, Kerbala is noted for a battle in 680AD when Hussein and his brother were killed and were after buried here. The original tomb was destroyed in 850AD but reconstructed in its present form in 979AD. A fire ravaged it in 1086AD and yet again it was repaired. Because of its Shia roots, the region maintained strong links with the Shias in Persia [Iran] and in the early part of the 20th Century, 75% of the population had Persian origins.

After the First World War, the British occupation saw to it that Iraqis born and bred were given special consideration and Persian domination ceased, forcing many to return to Persia. By the late 50s only 12% of the population was of Persian origin and they were offered and accepted Iraqi nationality.

Since the largely Sunni Baath Party came to power, this Shia stronghold was not given any favours, and attempts were made to kerb religious ceremonies, and non Iraqi Shia Moslems were banned from going there.

Certainly the place had a totally different feel to it than either Baghdad or Mosul. It was noticeable that most of the men wore the traditional

Arab clothing and all women wore the traditional black. Horse drawn cabs were more apparent than car taxis and there were many more street traders with mobile stalls. It was as I imagined Baghdad to be in the 40s and 50s before modernisation.

Our client had a small factory on an industrial area on the outskirts and was already finding demand exceeding his ability to produce.

These trips south of Baghdad meant I didn't have time to get to Mosul, and it was becoming apparent that two visits a year to Iraq were not enough to do all I wanted.

The doubts about the Non Aligned Conference were confirmed when it was cancelled during the summer because of the war. The Iranians had regained all the territory lost at the beginning of the war and were now actually on Iraqi soil with Basrah within shelling range.

I went back in November and found Baghdad operating as if nothing was happening out of the ordinary. Street lights were still off, but all hotels and public buildings were well lit. There was little military presence on the streets apart from anti aircraft gun emplacements on each bridge and on top of some buildings.

To my surprise, all the various projects, which had been under way for the conference, had been completed against all odds. The new airport "Saddam International" was open and the elaborate road network from the airport to central Baghdad was fully open. The accommodation blocks for the world's media, the conference centre and the two major hotels, the Sheraton and Meridian were all ready. Pity no one came to the party!

The Baghdad Trade Fair failed to lift the spirits and a general feeling of anticlimax and war weariness was everywhere.

In an attempt to retrieve the situation, the president was now making far more public appearances and attending medal ceremonies, all of which were faithfully recorded in the press and ad nauseum on TV. Large anti-Iran rallies were organised on Fridays after the morning prayers.

Many migrant workers had stayed on with companies, replacing Iraqi men who had been called up into the army. The age range for conscription had now been widened to all those born after 1948. To prevent Iraqi men travelling abroad to avoid call up, travel restrictions were in place and Iraqi businessmen could now only travel if they had a written invitation from an overseas company to do so. Needless to say I received several requests to send invitations which I was glad to do.

The curbs on spending were after all now starting to affect my customers and they were experiencing delays in getting import licences. Better things were promised for 1983. Few were optimistic.

I let January '83 pass by in the hope that licences would come through by the time I went back in February. No such luck however and our customers were starting to run out of raw materials as well as packaging and facing the prospect of shutting down their factories.

With no new projects being started, the number of cranes on the Baghdad skyline had declined considerably. Work on two new bridges across the Tigris was still going ahead and remarkably, drilling was taking place to explore the possibility of building a Baghdad Metro.

Iraq's oil exports had remained at 600,000 barrels a day through the Turkish pipeline up to the end of 1982 but now Turkey was demanding a higher tariff and Iraq had to reduce the output. An agreement had been signed in principle, with the old enemy Syria, to use an old pipeline but the final settlement had yet to be agreed. A new pipeline to the coast of Saudi Arabia was under construction, and was confidently expected to be completed by the end of the year.

Saudi Arabia had stated that whilst they were still willing to underpin finance for the war, they were not going to support the home economy. So with the situation regarding Iraq's main source of income unclear, industry was going to have to wait to get its finance.

It must have been very shameful for Saddam, but for the first time Iraq turned to the International Monetary Fund and negotiated a

$5,000,000 loan. A loan deal was also negotiated with France. The Iraq Dinar was devalued by 10% against the dollar and all foreign exchange deals were carefully scrutinised by the central bank.

On top of the cancellation of the conference, this financial crisis meant that Saddam's standing in the Arab world sank even lower than before.

The war, of course, was still uppermost in people's minds and was having a sapping effect on life in Baghdad. In the evenings the streets were far less busy and cafés and shops were closed early. The frequency of taxis and cars carrying simple wooden coffins draped with an Iraqi flag was all too apparent, and further evidence that the war was being fought out fiercely at the front. Altogether it was a gloomy start to the year but I felt it necessary to let customers know that I would be back in April. This was no time to cut and run.

On my April '83 visit, I was joined for a few days by one of our company's technical staff. Mike was very experienced in the working of packaging machines. Many of these were now not functioning very well due to non expert operators. I didn't have the time to spend sorting out these matters and we were getting complaints about our packaging not working properly. Mike's assistance was invaluable and the company had agreed that he or his colleague Barry would accompany me occasionally as I was going to increase my visits to four a year. To be fair, neither Mike or Barry were keen to go. Mike, in particular, professed he had little time for the Middle East, but in reality, apart from doing an excellent job, I think he enjoyed the experience. Barry on the other hand, didn't and only came with me twice although he too did a good job which was appreciated by our customers.

During March some licences were issued but only for a proportion of customer's actual requirements, often as little as 15%. We did our best to get orders shipped quickly by road via Turkey and most managed to keep going albeit at a reduced rate. This caused a shortage of biscuits in the market especially as much of the production was sent to the army. One of our customers had to supply more special high nutritional biscuits for the army and we had to supply the packaging.

With limited production taking place, it was a good time for my colleague Mike to look at the various packaging operations and advise correct procedures to cut down on wastage.

I had been able to get rooms in the new Palestine Meridian. I had received a loyalty card having stayed in their hotels elsewhere in the Middle East and this worked wonders. I was able to use this hotel on nearly every visit afterwards. After a day travelling around Baghdad and beyond, in and out of factories, it was good to get back to my room and have a proper shower. I also discovered that it had a tennis court on the roof and I was able to join in some good sets with some Japanese men.

The hotel's location next to the gardens bordering the Tigris meant that at lunchtimes, when siestas were being taken, I could sit in the gardens to write reports or read a book. I noticed that other seats were occupied by young men and women keeping a respectful distance between themselves, mindful of the police patrols regularly patrolling the gardens.

In the evenings, if free, Mike and I would go for a walk around the local area. One evening, walking past one of the Government buildings, we noticed a man in civilian clothes standing guard at the entrance. He was carrying a rifle and was in an animated conversation with a young man and as we approached he stopped us. "Are you English?" he said. Somewhat worried, I replied "Yes," wondering if we were in some sort of prohibited zone. "Can you answer a question for me?" he said in perfect English. "What is the rule in the English Language regarding the silent 't' as in the word 'often'?"

Mike and I looked at each other perplexed. Thought processes took a few seconds to click in. I thought to myself I do pronounce the 't' so I said "English is a pretty crazy language and it depends on your accent and where you live."

To my relief the man said "This is exactly what I have been telling my student". It turned out that he was an English teacher at a local college and was on home guard duty.

There weren't many Iraqi visitors to London during the summer. Travel and currency restrictions meant that many had to remain in Iraq and couldn't escape the summer heat.

With the war now passing its 3rd anniversary, frantic efforts were still being made to shore up the economy. A number of countries including Japan, Turkey, Jordan, Egypt, Rumania and Bulgaria had accepted two year deferred payment terms. A British company, John Laings, who were building a water treatment centre had also accepted long term credit. The pressure was on for other suppliers to do the same. A high level delegation from Iraq came to London in October to negotiate extended terms of between 180 and 360 days with UK banks, not good news for British companies.

As for imports, priority was being given to foodstuffs and raw materials for food processing plants. No new machinery was allowed and even spare parts were hard to get licences for.

Completion of the pipeline to Saudi Arabia had run into difficulties, and was not now expected to be finished until the end of 1985 or even 1986. With the Syrian pipeline still closed, there was no option but to pump through Turkey and pay the increased tariff. Production was boosted to 900,000 barrels a day.

Our customers quickly fell into two groups. In the end, nearly all the biscuit manufacturers got 100% of their allocation because of demand from the army and because most of the raw materials could be bought locally. Confectionery manufacturers however, were only getting 15% to 30%. The sting in the tail was that there was now a 10% tax levied on all payments for the war effort.

There was still plenty for me to do, so I went again towards the end of November, only 6 weeks after my October visit. Some customers were getting the impression that I was living in Baghdad!

In an effort to boost the President's popularity, Iraq TV now had an hour long programme every night showing Saddam Hussein meeting deputations from outlying parts of Iraq which had come to present their gifts of gold and other valuables for the war effort. Whole families seemed to be there in the Presidential Palace; fathers, mothers, old people, young children and babies. Having made their presentation to the President, a sort of impromptu concert took place. Speeches were read out, young people read poems and sang anti-Khomeini songs all followed by tumultuous applause and hugs and kisses from the President.

The giving of gold then became a national event and the larger donors had their photograph taken with the President.

It was all a sign of how bad Iraq's financial situation had become. The country's financial reserves normally stood at between 30 and 35 billion dollars but had now fallen to between $2-3 billion. Pressure was put on OPEC to allow Iraq to increase production and to raise the price of oil but this was resisted fiercely by the Gulf States.

To maintain the austerity programme, a bartering system had been introduced. Turkey was supplying flour, sugar and other foodstuffs in exchange for oil. A similar deal had also been agreed with Brazil in exchange for VW Passat cars.

The diplomatic activity to secure extended credit had produced a list of "favoured nations". This consisted of the whole of the Communist Eastern Bloc, the rest of the Arab world, but more significantly as far as I was concerned, the UK with a £250 million long term credit. Austria, France and West Germany had also been included on the list.

The sphere of war now extended along the whole border, from north to south, and with both sides bogged down in the south, the main activity now switched to the north. Iraqi TV was still showing the President attending medal ceremonies and pictures from the battle fronts claiming Iraqi victories. Independent research revealed that 12,000 Iranians had been killed in the last month alone, whilst the overall casualty rate was now reckoned to be over 300,000 killed on both sides.

Another possible problem was that Jordan, Iraq's greatest ally, was facing internal difficulties with the PLO threatening to destabilise the country. Iraq faced the prospect of having to go to Jordan's aid if an uprising occurred.

What a year this had been for President Saddam Hussein. Facing public disillusionment with the war, the financial problems mounting, having to hold out a begging bowl to take his people's gold, he was no longer the strong man of the Middle East.

# 12

## GOOD ADVICE IS BEYOND PRICE  LATIN PROVERB

One of the best bits of advice I ever received was from someone very experienced in Middle Eastern matters. He told me always "to expect the unexpected". By 1984, I had been travelling around the Middle East and Iraq in particular, for almost 10 years. Every time I came to Iraq, there was always a surprise in store, sometimes good and sometimes not so good, although that wasn't often.

Nineteen-eighty-four was one of those years. My first visit in February coincided with a big Iranian push on all fronts and the atmosphere in Baghdad was very tense. Security was very tight and large blocks of concrete had been placed around Government and other public buildings as well as the major hotels for fear of suicide bombings. We had a couple of air raid warnings but the targets were at Baquba, 25km away where three people were killed. Iranian dead and prisoners of war were found to be carrying white plastic keys, which they had been given as their entry to Paradise.

When I came a couple of months later in April, I was at first refused entry at Saddam International Airport. Worryingly, my passport was taken away along with that of another British traveller. We were put in a small room with no explanation and after a very long hour, our passports were returned and we went on our way. Registering at the British Embassy was now a necessity. I was told that our short "arrest" was probably due to a broadcast on the BBC World Service. A reporter in Cairo had obtained a copy of a US report on Human Rights violations in Iraq. As a result Iraq had jammed broadcasts and an anti-British campaign had been started in the press and on TV. This continued throughout my stay, not that I encountered any hostility from my customers, the opposite in fact.

Moustafa, our agent, had really got the hang of things and had lined up lots more people for me to see. These were in the Jamila district, the other side of the Army Canal. Here were many smaller companies making biscuits and especially wafers. I would never have found them without Moustafa's help, but very often they found us. Quite frequently, someone would come in from a nearby unit and ask us to go there when we had finished our meeting. It became obvious that they all communicated with each other and knew each other's business. Our packaging was attracting a lot of favourable attention and no one wanted to be second best.

I also went down to Musayib to try and find out why the owner had suddenly stopped communicating with us and had placed his orders elsewhere. The reason soon became apparent. In the summer of 1983, he had visited London and I had met him there. During our meeting he had asked me if I could lend him £500 for him to give to a student relative studying in London. At that time I didn't have that sort of money and had to say no. He had taken this as a personal insult because he thought I was the owner of the packaging company. Moustafa explained that I was merely of lowly status and immediately there was a profuse apology and smiles and handshakes all round!

Another strange meeting took place when I was in Mosul. Khalid told me that there was a local tribal leader who wanted to meet me, but on my own. I was collected from the hotel in a pick up vehicle and driven several miles away from the city to a small village. There, I was shown into a square, flat-roofed white building and then into a room bare except for seats around the four walls with the door in the corner. I waited for several minutes before a man came in dressed in the traditional Kurdish garb. He was flanked by two men carrying automatic weapons, and another man who acted as an interpreter.

After the normal courtesies and customary tea, I was questioned for the best part of an hour, about the feasibility of setting up a snack food factory. Fortunately, because of my experience of dealing with similar projects in the Gulf, I had a good idea of the costs involved and useful contacts for him to make. I was driven back to the hotel and neither Khalid or I ever heard any more.

Mike, our technical expert, was with me on one of my 1984 trips and we had a couple of strange complaints to sort out. One related to a salty cracker type biscuit, which our customer told us was going soft in our packaging. This was a real puzzle because we had supplied a special protective material. We went to the factory and observed the baking and packaging process. We examined the seals and the packs were definitely airtight. We followed the packs to the area where they were being put into cardboard containers ready for despatch to the market. As we watched, we noticed the packer sticking a pin into the pack so that he could get the air out and more packs into the container!

Another complaint from another company concerned small packs of biscuits sticking together. When we investigated this we found that the cooling belt taking the biscuits from the oven to the packaging machine had been removed and biscuits were coming straight out from the oven into the packaging machines which had been moved next to the oven. The temperature of the biscuits was melting the protective coating on the packaging. We got the cooling belt put back and the problem went away.

I also took Mike with me to Mosul. We travelled by taxi and I persuaded the driver to divert off the main Baghdad-Mosul highway and go to the ancient ruins of Hatra. They are 15 miles from the highway and Hatra is 180 miles from Baghdad and 68 miles from Mosul. On arrival we found a gatekeeper/guard, paid a small entrance fee and found ourselves the only people there! It is an amazing site and when things normalise will prove to be one of the great tourist sites.

Hatra was founded by the Assyrians in the 3rd century BC as a religious and trading centre. Later it was the capital of a series of Arab cities as far as Petra in Jordan. The Romans weren't able to take it and it survived various sieges from invading armies until it fell in 241AD following an act of treachery by An-Nadira, daughter of King Sanatruq II. She allowed entrance to the city by the army of Shapur I head of the Sassanid Empire. He killed her father and married her, but she too was killed by him later. The city was destroyed and has lain in ruins ever since.

The site is very impressive. The reason why it was able to withstand several sieges was a system of impregnable walls surrounding the city. There were two, an outer and inner wall, 4 miles in circumference and connected by 160 towers and four gateways corresponding to the points on a compass.

The Great Temple was built with columns up to 30 metres high. Many other smaller temples were built for the worship of various Gods and several statues still remain. The dry atmosphere has preserved the site well and it is easy to see how the architectural style influenced Greek architecture. We only had time to spend an hour there and I would have liked to spend longer for there was much to see.

Whilst in Mosul, I took Mike to see the site of Ninevah. When walking down a street nearby, Mike suddenly stopped and headed for the side of the road where a small pump was working. On close examination Mike identified it as a Lister pump from Stroud, and a plate gave a date of 1934. A small group of men and boys gathered round wondering what we were up to. We made signs indicating our appreciation of the machine which seemed to please them and there were handshakes all round. They must have thought we were mad!

The war now entered its 5$^{th}$ year and showed no sign of ending. I suppose that up until now I had felt somewhat detached from the situation. After all, I could escape back to the UK after a few days. With Baghdad relatively safe, I did not feel in any danger. Even the sight of coffins on top of cars had become so commonplace as almost to lose impact. The mood of my customers was becoming increasingly gloomy. Many I could now count as friends and I knew that life was becoming very difficult for them.

One evening, the reality of war struck home. I was invited to a meal at a customer's home. I had met him 12 months earlier and he had introduced me to his family. His son had recently qualified as a doctor and I guess he would be around 28 years old and was shortly due to go to serve in the army. This evening, he was home on a 48 hour pass. If I had met him elsewhere, I would not have recognised him. He looked nearer 60 than 30. His hair had gone completely grey, his face was gaunt, and he had lost a lot of weight. He didn't say much except to explain that he had been serving in the medical unit on the front line in the south and had to deal with horrific injuries and the results of chemical warfare on both sides.

This image certainly brought home to me the horrors of war and was to come to mind a year later.

In a surprising diplomatic move, the U.S.A. established a full diplomatic mission in Iraq. The U.S.A. had no love for Khomeini and had recently suffered acute embarrassment when captured Iranians were found to be carrying American-made weapons. Although they had originated in the U.S.A. they had found their way to Iran via third or even fourth parties. It was felt that this new development would cut off the supply of weapons to Iran and force them to the negotiating table.

The establishment of a U.S. Embassy heralded the arrival of a trade delegation. I was in the Bunnia office when a group breezed in. They ignored everyone else in the office and kept calling Mr. Al Bunnia "Wayhab" which I thought very disrespectful. His full name is Abdul Wahab al Bunnia and Wahab is pronounced with a short "a". As usual with any visitors, they were treated with courtesy but I don't think their brashness gained them many friends.

Moustafa too had his own surprise. With the two major hotels, Sheraton and Meridian, now open, he was keen to try out the restaurant in the Sheraton and invited me to join him and his wife for dinner one evening. Seeing a fish dish on the western style menu, Moustafa placed his order, thinking perhaps of the huge Masgouf river fish served in Iraqi homes. The look on his face when the cover was lifted to reveal a small fillet, said it all. For an Iraqi appetite, it was probably two or three mouthfuls!

The entertainers that evening had a surprise coming to them. I had been to Iraqi restaurants, where perhaps a singer or belly dancer would perform. If the act went well, Iraqi men would show their appreciation by tucking Dinar notes into the male performer's pocket or in the case of the belly dancer...!

The Sheraton that evening had a trio of European young ladies playing a selection of light classical music. They were elegantly dressed in ball gowns and the music went down well with the diners. After much applause, men were going up and tucking notes wherever they could, leaving the girls blushing furiously. Womanfully, they struggled on and completed their programme, retiring quickly at the end!

A people's army for men over 45 was entrusted with the job of guarding public buildings. Many were worried about this development because they feared they might eventually get sent to the front. There was evidence that the Iranians were trying out a new tactic of sending old men and young boys ahead of any advance, to trigger off land mines and so clear the way for advancing troops. A grisly plan indeed!

Our customers were getting used to seeing me four times a year. More than one actually thought I was now resident in Baghdad. As a result, I was getting lots of invitations to meals at their homes, so many in fact that I just couldn't fit them all in and had to promise "next time". I am not a big eater and five consecutive nights of Masgouf was hard to handle! One client, when I declined an evening invitation, insisted that I go and have lunch with him. He took Moustafa and I to a Quzi restaurant where lamb or mutton is boiled and served with rice mixed with almonds, raisins and spices. It was very tasty but the portions were huge and I knew I had another Masgouf to tackle that evening. The hospitality and friendship I was shown by all made my visits all the more pleasant despite the difficult situation everyone was living with.

Hatra: Great Temple

Hatra: South Gate

Hatra: Eagle Bas Relief

Hatra: Statues

Hatra: Queen Abbu

Hatra: Statue of Queen Abbu

103

Hatra: Musician relief

Hatra: Temple arch

Hatra: The Great Temple

Hatra: Wall carving with architect's inscription

Mosul

Mosul: Nomad's encampment

Mosul: Nomads with sheep

Mosul: Sheep and lambs

Mosul: The Great Nurid Mosque

Sheep sale at Baiji

City walls, Nineveh

Nineveh: Reconstructed city gate

105

Statue of a king, Nineveh museum

Wall relief, Nineveh

Iraqi regional costumes

More regional costumes

107

# 13

## AT THE GOING DOWN OF THE SUN, AND IN THE MORNING, WE WILL REMEMBER THEM.
ROBERT LAURENCE BINYON

During one visit in 1985, I was introduced to a period of British history, which I was totally unaware of. Moustafa and I were asked to go to Kut, some 100 miles south east of Baghdad. It was further evidence that industry was spreading around the country.

It was not a particularly interesting journey. Mile after mile of flat, parched, featureless landscape, with the monotony only broken by seeing the nests of cranes in the electricity pylons which lined the road. The true relevance of this scene was to become apparent to me later.

Kut, capital of the Wasit Province, seemed to have little to commend it. A city of some 400,000 people, it is situated on the left bank of the Tigris in a mainly agricultural area. Our client's new biscuit factory was on a site close to the river in some attractive gardens. After a productive meeting, we were invited to have lunch in a small marquee set up in the gardens. Needless to say it was a fish meal, but very enjoyable. I could not help noticing several scrawny cats hovering by the entrance. No sooner had we left the table, than they leapt onto it to get at the remains of the fish.

Our hosts asked me what I knew about the British Army in Kut during the First World War and I had to admit I knew nothing at all. They told me that in 1916, Kut had been the centre of a major battle and siege, and that there was a large military cemetery here. When they offered to take me there, I jumped at the chance. On the way we passed a barrage across the Tigris which had been constructed by British Army engineers. I noticed two Victorian-type lamp standards positioned on the barrage looking very out of place.

I wondered if they had been some kind of joke because I couldn't see what function they had.

Kut Military Cemetery contains the graves of 420 British and Indian servicemen who perished here in 1916. The cemetery was well maintained by a local man who was only too pleased for me to look around. I took some photographs and later sent them to the Imperial War Graves Commission who were pleased to have them as this area was out of bounds to British Embassy staff at that time.

I resolved to find out more about the happenings in 1916 little realising what an awful story would be revealed to me in the process. For a full, very descriptive history, I can really recommend a book by Ron Wilcox called *Battles on the Tigris*. This gives a full and graphic account of the whole campaign.

At the outbreak of the First World War, an expeditionary force was sent from India to protect British owned oil fields in Persia. Iraq, or Mesopotamia as the region was known, was then occupied by the Turks as part of the Ottoman Empire. The force was Anglo-Indian comprising of 1,000 British and 4,000 Indian troops. It arrived at Seni Yeh at the head of the Persian Gulf at the end of November 1914. Basrah was the first objective, and it was quickly taken after the Turks evacuated. Having established a base there, a force under the command of General Charles Townshend moved north using river transport. In September 1915 they attacked the Turks at Amara. Townshend's relatively small force, two thirds of whom were of Indian nationality, was the 6th Poona Division. The Turkish opposition, with German officers, outnumbered them and were better equipped. Nevertheless, showing great bravery and determination they not only took Amara, but then continued to advance. After a further three days of fierce fighting they captured Kut. Here they established a base waiting for reinforcements and better equipment to come from Basrah. This did not happen.

After nine months Townshend was ordered to push further northwards and got as far as Ctesiphon, some 90 miles up river. Even though they were outnumbered 5-1, they won a famous battle, but with lack of supplies, particularly drinking water, he was forced to pull back to Kut. Baghdad had been tantalisingly close and with the right support from Basrah he could have taken it.

The Turks had sent reinforcements following the defeat at Ctesiphon, and Townshend's men had to fight a rearguard action all the way back to Kut. They finally made it back to Kut in December 1915.

With a U bend in the river Tigris, Kut was effectively on a peninsular and the pursuing Turkish army quickly sealed off the northern land area, thus trapping Townshend and his men in the city as well as all the local inhabitants. The cavalry section under the command of Colonel Gerard Leachman did manage to break out but the bulk of the force had no choice but to prepare for a siege and hope that a relief force would free them.

In the meantime, the Turks, under the German command of Baron Von Der Goltz, anticipated the arrival of a relieving force and dug in around the river banks opposite Kut and brought in heavy artillery.

It doesn't appear that the seriousness of Townshend's position was fully realised at first, and by the time a force was sent to try and relieve the siege, the Turks were well in control and repulsed all attempts. Such was the ferocity of the fighting, that some 23,000 British and Indian men were lost, the worst single loss of life outside of the European campaign.

Aircraft were used to try and drop supplies into Kut but the amount they could carry was so small as to make virtually no difference. Also the planes were easy targets and several were shot down. German planes attached to the Turkish Army were used to bomb Kut. A makeshift hospital which had a large red cross on its roof was also targeted.

General Townshend was able to maintain radio contact with the Command HQ in Basrah and advised them that he only had sufficient rations to last until early April. Not only did he have to consider his troops, but also 20,000 locals. He did his best to maintain morale, and there is no doubt that his men held him in high regard. Amongst his personal possessions he had a wind up gramophone and a few records, which he played regularly for the men. He even requested that a supply of gramophone needles be included in one of the aircraft drops.

Late January and the month of February had a heavy rainfall which hampered rescue attempts. They were subjected to daily bombardments and sniper fire. By early March, the shortage of fresh fruit and vegetables had caused many cases of scurvy among the men. As sanitary conditions deteriorated, cases of dysentery and gastro enteritis increased and many died. This coupled with the death rate from the daily attacks had a very debilitating effect on the men.

Action against the Turks was limited to sniper fire but of course fire was returned and the casualty rate soared. Death and injury amongst the local population was also on the increase and there was a danger that they would attempt to take over the garrison.

With the weather improving, one final attempt was made to get through and deliver supplies. A river boat, the Julnar, managed to navigate the first part of the river bend despite machine gun attacks. It was then struck by a shell and ran aground and was captured.

With no hope of relief, and with food stocks exhausted, the men now killed the horses and mules for their meat. General Townshend advised HQ of this now impossible position and asked for permission to surrender.

Diplomatic efforts were made by three British emissaries, including T.E Lawrence, but the Turks were in no mood to make any sort of compromise.

The surrender of Kut took place on the 29th April 1916. During the siege, some 4,000 British and Indian men had been killed or died of wounds or diseases. The attempts to rescue them had claimed around 23,000 lives whilst the Turks had lost over 10,000 men and officers.

I am writing this on Remembrance Sunday 2008 and what has started to become clear to me is the sheer scale of the fatalities at Kut. What is also clear is that for many there is no known grave. Turkish and

German casualties aside, the total loss of the Commonwealth Forces in Iraq was 17,805 British and 36,249 Indian men. Besides the 420 graves at Kut, there are graveyards and memorials throughout Iraq at Baghdad, Mosul, Basrah, Alwiya, Amara and Habanniyah. No doubt all the names of those who died are on war memorials up and down the United Kingdom and are honoured on Remembrance Day on the 11th of November.

What followed the surrender of Kut must rank as one of the darkest chapters of British military history. The sick and wounded were allowed to be taken by river boat down river to Basrah and were then sent to India. I suppose they were the lucky ones.

General Townshend was taken up river to be interned as a P.O.W. in Turkey. Before he left, he was given assurances by the Turkish Commander, Khalil Pasha, that the remaining British and Indian men, numbering about 2,000, would be treated properly. General Townshend had told Khalil Pasha, that the men were too weak to march due to the starvation diet they had been on. He was again assured that the men would be transported by boat to Baghdad and then by trucks to camps in Southern Turkey where the climate would be beneficial to their recovery. Townshend himself was offered the chance to join the wounded on the trip to Basrah, but declined and opted for captivity.

The Turkish clearout of Kut was quick and merciless. The men were immediately force marched to Shamron 8 miles to the north. Even in this short distance around 300 died of gastro enteritis. No proper burials took place and bodies were left where they fell to rot. Their captors then realised that the rest stood no chance of reaching Baghdad, and allowed some provisions to be sent in. It was however too little, too late. At this stage, any remaining officers were separated from the men and taken by boat to Baghdad although most were as sick as the their men.

By the end of April and the beginning of May the temperature was reaching well over 30°C. The men, guarded by Turkish and Kurdish soldiers, were marched north. They were beaten if they stopped and as each mile passed, more fell dying. Their bodies were stripped of clothing and anything else their captors thought worth taking. No burials took place.

The march to Baghdad took 8½ days with death stalking the half-naked, starved men all the way. Guards regularly stole the men's meagre rations and beat them if they resisted. Thinking back, that flat barren landscape between Baghdad and Kut took us just 2½ hours to travel and all the way must now hide the remains of many of General Townshend's men.

In Baghdad, they were paraded, shuffling through the streets. With the temperature now in the mid 30s, around 350 men were too sick to march any further. A makeshift camp was set up on the banks of the Tigris and following some diplomatic exchanges, a deal was struck whereby these very ill men could be transported down river to Basrah in exchange for 350 Turkish prisoners of war.
Full censorship was in place, and no one was allowed to report on the terrible treatment they had received or the conditions that the remaining men were facing.

The rest of the men still standing were herded into trucks and taken to Samarra, 70 miles north. They then faced a march of 500 miles to Turkey. Their treatment did not improve and in Ron Wilcox's book there are graphic details of the cruelty involved. Of the men captured at Kut, only 900 survived and many of these died later as a result of their treatment in captivity.

The surrender at Kut caused many questions to be asked in parliament and Lord Kitchener was obliged to make this statement to the House of Lords on 4th May 1916.

> MY LORDS
>
> I am glad that the Noble and Gallant Lord has afforded me this opportunity of paying a tribute to General Townshend and his troops, whose dogged determination and splendid courage have earned for them so honourable a record.
>
> It is well known how, after a series of brilliantly fought engagements, General Townshend decided to hold the strategically important position at Kut-el-Amara, and it will not be forgotten that his disposition for the defences of that place were so excellent and so complete that the enemy,

notwithstanding large numerical superiority, was wholly unable to penetrate his lines.

Noble Lords will not fail to realise how tense was the strain borne by those troops who for more than 20 weeks held to their posts under conditions of abnormal climatic difficulty, and on rations calculated for protraction to the furthest possible period until imminent starvation itself compelled the capitulation of this gallant garrison, which consisted of 2,970 British and some 6,000 Indian troops including followers.

General Townshend and his troops in their honourable captivity will have the satisfaction of knowing that, in the opinion of their comrades, which I think I may say this House and the country fully share, they did all that was humanly possible to resist to the last, and that their surrender reflects no discredit on themselves or on the record of the British and Indian armies.

Every effort was of course made to relieve the beleaguered force, and I am not travelling beyond the actual facts in saying that to the adverse elements alone was due the denial of success; the constant rain and consequent floods not only impeding the advance but compelling – in lieu of turning movements – direct attacks on an almost impossible narrow front. No praise would seem extravagant for the troops under Sir Percy Lake and Sir George Gorringe, and that they did not reap the fruit of their courage and devotion is solely due to the circumstances which fought against them.

The last message sent by General Townshend from Kut was addressed in these terms:-

"We are pleased to know that we have done our duty, and recognise that our situation is one of the fortunes of war. We thank you and General Gorringe and all the ranks of the Tigris force for the great efforts you have made to save us"

> I think the House, no less that the country at large, will endorse these words, and I am sure that those who held – and those who strained every nerve to relieve Kut, have alike earned our admiration and gratitude.

A full enquiry was held at a later stage into the circumstances of the surrender. No doubt these days the words "cover up" would spring to mind in relation to Lord Kitchener's statement. What should be remembered first of all is that the Tigris force was sent by the Indian Government at the request of the British Government. It was from the outset numerically less than the forces it faced and was seriously worse equipped. This scenario was quickly realised by the command base at Basrah and repeated requests were sent to London for reinforcements and more equipment. These were initially refused by Lord Kitchener, who did not want to take anything, or anybody away from the Western Front. Blame and recriminations for the Kut surrender were passed back and forth between the British and Indian military and seriously affected Anglo-British relations. General Townshend, following his release after the armistice, went to live in Paris. He was criticised unfairly in some sections of the press. He was retired on half pay and never given another command. He died in 1924 aged 63.

Kut was eventually recaptured in February 1917. The British government, still smarting over the surrender, at last sent men and supplies to reinforce the remaining army in southern Mesopotamia. The advance north was now properly backed up with the necessary supply chain, not that progress was swift. The Turks proved to be a determined fighting force and heavy casualties were suffered on both sides. In fact on the Allies side, the proportion of those in the battles who died was said to be greater than that on the Western Front.

Baghdad was taken and the advance north took in several major battles up to Mosul where Turkish resistance ended just before the armistice was signed.

In the aftermath, it was found that of all the men who actually reached Turkish prisoner of war camps, more than half died there.

The cemetery at Kut contains the graves of only 420 British and Indian men. One grave in particular caught my attention. It was of Private 2253 Edward Henry Stone D. C. M. who died on the 18th March 1916 aged 26. This was the date of my father's 8th birthday. My research, courtesy of the Keep Military Museum in Dorchester and the National Archives, records that Private Stone was born in Portland, Dorset and joined the 1st/5th Battalion of the Devonshire Regiment in 1915. He was then attached to the Dorsetshire Regiment and sent to India and thence to Mesopotamia as part of the expeditionary force.

During the siege of Kut, he was mentioned in dispatches and then awarded the Distinguished Conduct Medal for gallantry. The award was made posthumously on the 2nd December 1917 and it was recorded that he died of wounds on the 18th March 1916, just one of many brave men.

The graveyard at Kut has fared badly since 1990. The local caretaker, who I met, was not paid after the first Gulf War started. Saddam Hussein ordered that the site be used as a rubbish dump as punishment for Britain's involvement in the war. In 2003, after the US and British troops had overthrown Saddam Hussein, a party of American marines carefully set about restoring the cemetery. All the rubbish was cleared with the help of some local people and a new central cross was made and erected on the site of the old one shown in my photograph. When the work was completed a special rededication ceremony was held attended by US marines, British soldiers, Kut city officials and local townspeople. Unfortunately the raising of the Union Jack and the generally high profile nature of the ceremony angered a lot of the local population who felt that greater priority should have been given to restoring power and food supplies. Riots took place during the course of which the graveyard including the new cross was vandalised. It was admitted that, with hindsight, too much publicity had been given to the event.

I believe the other military graveyards throughout Iraq suffered under Saddam after 1990 but no doubt in time all will be restored to their proper state. A plaque was put on the new cross at Kut. The message read "When you go home, tell them of us and say: For your tomorrow we gave our today".

The 90th anniversary of the armistice has just passed by with all the emphasis of the horrors of the Western Front, not that I would want that played down in any way. I do feel however that the Mesopotamian campaign deserves greater recognition and I wonder if it is ignored because of the surrender at Kut.

Kut War Cemetery

Kut Military Cemetery

Kut Grave of Private Stone DCM

Saddam the Leader, Baghdad

Train near Kerbala

Horse drawn taxi, Kerbala

A Mullah, Kerbala

Holy Shrine of Imam Abbas, Kerbala

All aboard the bus from Baghdad to Amman

Cake seller

Baghdad Observer

Baghdad Observer headlines

Badhdad bus terminal

Imam Abbas Shrine, Kerbala

Imam Abbas Shrine, Kerbala

Palestine Meridian Hotel, Baghdad

Rashid Street, Baghdad

Saddoun Street, Baghdad

River Tigris, Baghdad

Seventh Day Adventist Church, Baghdad

St Joseph's Catholic Church, Baghdad

Street café, Baghdad

Shoeshine boys, Baghdad

# 14

## ACTIONS SPEAK LOUDER THAN WORDS 20$^{th}$ Cent

If the good citizens of Baghdad needed reminding that there was a war on, then they certainly got one on the 20$^{th}$ March 1985, just one month before my second visit of the year in April.

By now the damaged power supply network, which had been severely disrupted at Nasriyah early in the war, had been repaired and Baghdad was functioning almost normally. There were no restrictions on lights. The Iraqi Air Force now held supremacy in the skies and Baghdad was supposed to be protected by a sophisticated anti-missile system.

However in the middle of the night on March 20$^{th}$, Iranian missiles struck Baghdad. The first struck the tallest building in the city – the Rafidain Bank and blew out the top five floors leaving just the steel framework. The bottom five floors were also severely damaged. Blast damage covered a wide area. Moustafa's office was directly opposite the bank and all the windows were blown out but thankfully no one was hurt. Half a mile away the Bunnia offices had windows broken. Other missiles landed at random over a two square mile area and it seemed a pure fluke that one had hit the Rafidain Bank. The theory was that they were aimed at the Presidential Palace but one hit an elevated section of the main highway to the east of Baghdad whilst two fell near the river. Another fell near a hospital and here several people were killed.

The psychological effect on the citizens of Baghdad must have pleased the Iranians for the Rafidain Bank was right in the heart of the commercial area and therefore seen by many thousands each day.

In an effort to restore the public's morale, a day of national celebration was organised for the president's 48th birthday on the 28th April. Large demonstrations were held with many street parades. In the evening there were street parties outside official buildings. Just up the road from where I was staying was an event held outside the traffic police's HQ. Here a huge birthday cake with 48 candles was centrepiece. A string orchestra played and all the police sang the Arabic version of *Happy Birthday* to the traditional tune.

A couple of days later on May 1st, more demonstrations and parades took place with an estimated 2 million people taking part. From early morning large decorated floats drawn by trucks or tractors arrived in Baghdad from all sides. All bore large pictures of Saddam Hussein. Iraqi TV showed nothing else all day.

Summer 1985 came and went with few visitors to the UK. This was because the Iraq Government had now placed more restrictions on businessmen travelling abroad. They could now only visit one country. This posed a real dilemma for many as they had suppliers in several European countries. The situation provided me with a very unusual experience.

One customer had machinery in his factory of East German origin and needed to go to East Berlin to negotiate the supply of spare parts. He also wanted more packaging material having obtained an import licence and asked me to meet him in East Berlin. This was a problem as at that time entry was not permitted. Germany was still partitioned and Berlin was divided by that infamous wall.

I went to the East German Embassy in London and at first they refused my request for a visa. I persisted and explained fully the reason and circumstances for the visit, and to cut a long story short, they agreed to issue me with a 24 hour visa, but with the proviso that they would arrange for a security man to meet me at West Berlin's Templehof Airport to escort me to East Berlin and the same procedure on the return.

On arrival at Templehof I was met by a large well built man holding a card with my name on. He was dressed in black and looked every inch a security guard. He drove a big black car and we went to

Checkpoint Charlie on the Berlin Wall. The wall didn't look that high to me, about 9 feet, but having passed security and gone to the other side I could see the rolls of barbed wire in front of it. Only the brave or foolhardy would have attempted to get over it. Not once did the man speak. It was very strange. He delivered me to the hotel where my customer was staying and where I also was booked in. He said something to the receptionist who told me he would be back next day to pick me up.

I finished my business that evening and next morning decided to venture out to see what the place was like. I can best describe it as bleak. West Berlin was bustling with people, well dressed and looking affluent. Mercedes and BMW cars were everywhere. In the street where I was there were few shops with nothing much in them. People looked pale and drawn. The few cars that were about were Trabants and Ladas all belching out smoke from their exhausts. A party of schoolchildren passed by heading for the nearby Brandenburg Gate. I tagged on behind and nobody seemed to mind, but I decided not to take any photographs.

That afternoon, dead on the dot, my "guard" collected me from the hotel and delivered me back to Templehof Airport, again not speaking a word. I thanked him but received no acknowledgement and off he drove. It had been a very odd 24 hours.

When I returned to Baghdad in September I was advised by the British Embassy that Iraq's financial position was looking very vulnerable indeed. Two large international repayments to Germany and Japan had been delayed and rescheduled due to a shortage of hard currency. The UK had not been affected so far but caution was urged.

Moustafa too was in a nervous state. Forty-five of the leading commission agents including Moustafa had been summoned to the import ministry at the end of August. They were told that it was assumed that each of them was keeping part of their commission outside Iraq. They were instructed, under threat of severe penalties, and I mean *severe*, to transfer all overseas funds back to Iraq and to close all accounts held there. Anyone not complying fully could expect the worst. This threat certainly frightened the life out of

Moustafa, who like everyone else had kept a small amount in the UK to tide him over on UK visits following the currency restrictions imposed by Iraq. As a result he had to transfer everything back in US dollars at a very disadvantageous rate. He was worried that there would be further repercussions. The news had also reached the ears of several customers who had similar arrangements and all were very nervous.

The war now entered its 6th year but no more missiles had landed. Fifteen in all had been fired but apart from the spectacular success at hitting the Rafidain Bank and the fatalities at the hospital. The rest had fallen without causing major damage.

The Iraqi harvest had been a good one but in order to raise foreign exchange, fresh produce was being exported to neighbouring Arab countries causing shortages in the local market.

Much to my surprise, major European airlines including British Airways, resumed direct flights to Baghdad. They still arrived and left at dead of night and suitcases had to be identified in darkness by the side of the aircraft before they were loaded into the plane's hold.

Nineteen-eighty-five ended on a high note however. Iraq became the 23rd country to qualify for the 1986 World Cup tournament in Mexico. In the final game in their group, they had to beat, arch rivals Syria. Two weeks earlier in Damascus, the game had ended 0–0. There was much recrimination because of the bad reception given to the Iraqi team, which was not allowed to bring any supporters. Syria refused to play the return match in Iraq because of the war so the fixture was transferred to Taif in Saudi Arabia. The Iraqi Air Force laid on 27 giant transport planes. Universities and colleges were emptied and with other men it was claimed that they transported 8,000 to the game.

The resulting 3–1 victory was greeted as if Iraq had won the World Cup itself. The streets were eerily quiet whilst the game was on. Cafés and restaurants were packed with people following the game on TV. After the game, people took to the streets in celebration, cheering and shouting wildly. A lot of small-arms fire could be heard.

This fillip to Iraq's morale could not have come at a better time as the war dragged on in its 6th year. Apart from reports of regular raids by planes on the Iranian oil base at Kharg Island which had stopped 90% of the oil flow, there was little other military information coming from the various fronts. It was rumoured that the Iranians were again massing for a major offensive in the south but Iraqi defences were well dug in and they had repulsed such attacks before. The war seemed to have settled into a pattern of cross border exchanges of shelling.

People I came into contact with were now very depressed and resigned to the war going on for the foreseeable future. Many had sons serving in the army and those sons still at school were being urged to study for all they were worth because it was only by passing examinations and going on to higher education that students could delay their military service.

The final section of the pipeline to Saudi Arabia had finally been completed and 400 to 500,000 barrels a day were now being pumped through, virtually doubling the country's output and bringing in much needed foreign exchange. This was certainly needed to take the pressure off outstanding loan deals. Iraq was still getting a favourable response from EEC members but the overall financial outlook was worrying. Our customers by the end of the year had no idea what import licences they would get in 1986.

# 15

## DEBT IS THE WORST POVERTY T. FULLER 1732

By the time of my first visit in February '86, the feel good factor created by the success of Iraq's football team and the extra revenue from the Saudi pipeline, had vanished. Oil prices had plummeted to as low as $15 a barrel and even though OPEC was allowing Iraq not to cut back its production, the resulting shortfall in income had forced a complete rethink of the budget for 1986. Our customers had been told to expect a 50% cut in their import licences. As a result, some customers had done barter deals with Turkish suppliers, which did not require a licence.

The anticipated Iranian offensive had not yet taken place and Iraq launched an offensive of its own, mainly led by the air force attacking military positions. It appeared that Iraq now had total supremacy in the air and could attack at will.

One concern was that Kurdish separatists, operating out of eastern Turkey with the backing of the Iranians, were causing problems in the north. Since one of the major regiments in the Iraq army was composed entirely of Kurdish soldiers, concerns were being expressed about their loyalty should things escalate in the north.

With the Kharg Island oil terminal at the northern end of the Gulf virtually out of action, the Iranians were now switching to a new terminal at Sirri Island at the southern end and out of range of Iraqi bombers.

In a surprise move, Iran mounted a counter offensive on the afternoon of Sunday 9th February. News of this was immediately broadcast, which was surprising. A meeting that had been arranged was cancelled and I found myself with a rare evening free.

I decided to go to the Anglican St George Church for the evening service. The church is situated in central Baghdad in Haifa Street very close to some Government ministry buildings. Building started in 1935 and it was dedicated on May 6th 1937. It is under the jurisdiction of the Anglican Bishop of Jerusalem but at this time there was no resident vicar. The service was well attended by mainly Europeans, many of whom seemed to have come from various embassies. The service was led by a lay reader from the British Embassy and followed the traditional Anglican evensong which, considering the situation we were all in and also my non-conformist background, seemed rather odd. Refreshments were served after the service but everyone, including me, was anxious to get back.

Travelling back to my hotel, the streets were very quiet and cafés were closing down early. For the next two days there were non-stop broadcasts but then, suddenly, there was a complete news blackout which only served to increase people's nervousness and general depression. By the time I left on the 13th, it had been announced that the attack had been repulsed on all fronts. The truth was that the Iranians had advanced deep into Iraq across the Shatt al Arab delta, and captured the Iraqi port of Fao.

Just before I left, Baghdad had suffered some very cold weather with gale force winds and severe thunderstorms. Even the new sewers and drainage systems could not cope, and many areas were flooded and there was plenty of mud.

By the time I returned in April, the world's financial institutions were casting nervous glances at Iraq's increasingly desperate financial position. Revenue from oil exports continued to be the main source of income but the fall in its price looked likely to last the rest of the year, thus casting doubt over Iraq's ability to repay long term loans.

During my stay, I was joined, for a couple of days by a colleague from another group company, which supplied unprinted material to the State owned tobacco company in Arbil. Since I had a customer in Kirkuk we decided to make a joint visit. Since Arbil is some 210 miles from Baghdad, an early start was required and we left Baghdad at 6.00am.

Moustafa's car was more comfortable than the taxis and we made good time, arriving in Arbil just after 10.30am. I would have liked to have had a good look around this city, which is claimed to be the oldest continuously inhabited city in the world dating back to 2000BC, but there wasn't time.

The first thing which one couldn't help noticing was Arbil Castle, high on the hill overlooking the city. In Assyrian and Babylonian times Arbil was known as Arba Ilu [The Four Gods] and over the centuries it had flourished as a religious centre, fortress, trading region and was now an important Kurdish City.

Alas we had a meeting to get to at the tobacco factory. We were shown into the ground floor office of the company's buyer and my colleague carried out his negotiations. At 11.00am precisely, a loud volley of gun shots rang out and the buyer immediately dived under his desk. We quickly followed suit!

A man came rushing into the office, and told us not to be alarmed. It was Saddam Hussein's birthday and the gunfire was a salute in his honour. The buyer told us that his reaction was as a result of some skirmishes a few days earlier when there had been a raid by Kurdish separatists. The poor chap was very embarrassed and apologised profusely.

The meeting over, we headed south for Kirkuk, a distance of 56 miles. We had been warned that because of the recent Kurdish separatists' raids, a curfew would come into place at 4.00pm and we would need to be out of the governorate well in time to avoid any problems.

Arriving in the area around lunchtime, the most obvious features were the oil installations – Iraq's lifeblood. The flames burning off the gas made a spectacular sight. It is said that before oil was discovered, the whole area had fissures through which gas seeped and regularly caught fire.

It is also thought that this is the site where in the Old Testament, Daniel, Shadrach, Meshach and Abednego endured and emerged unscathed from their ordeal by fire ordered by King Nebuchadnezzar for refusing to worship the king's God.

Kirkuk also has an ancient history but didn't have the importance of the other cities until oil was discovered in 1927. Now of course it is arguably the most important.

Our customer was anxious to provide a lunch but Moustafa explained that we had a 70 mile journey to do to get to the next governorate and he wanted to be away not later than 2.00pm. Such is the nature of Iraqi hospitality that our customer was disappointed not to be able to entertain us in the manner he would have liked. He did understand the problem and he provided a pile of sandwiches together with tea and coffee.

We left promising to spend longer with him next time if conditions allowed. Fortunately there was little traffic on the road from Kirkuk to Tikrit where we joined the Baghdad–Mosul highway. The road from Kirkuk was almost dead straight and every mile there was a gun emplacement on top of a mound of earth, evidence of the tight security in the area. Moustafa comfortably made it to Tikrit well before 4.00pm and we observed the banners, flags and bunting which had been put out, not to greet us but to celebrate Saddam Hussein's birthday. This was his home town, and large pictures of him were everywhere.

The economic position was still very confused and during the summer, the Iraq Government introduced several measures to try and reduce the flow of hard currency out of the country. The transfer of money by ex pat workers was severely restricted. Foreign travel for businessmen was now limited to three days in one country only, which made overseas trips almost impossible. Grants for overseas scholarships were curtailed. Those foreign companies tendering for public sector projects were told that they had to accept long term payments with a minimum of two years. Many major European companies had turned their back on Iraq.

Our customers had been instructed to insist on 12 months credit but the UK banks, which were handling Iraq credits, would only support 6 months. Even now customers had no idea how much they would be allowed to import. Many were only operating for 2 or 3 days a week and our order book was looking a bit thin. The question of overseas accounts had now reached the owners of Iraqi businesses and one of my customers was under arrest, news which all knew about.

The restrictions on the transfer of money by ex pats had led to thousands of Egyptians deciding to return home and as a result, all approaches to the airport were blocked by long queues of men, most of whom had to wait 3 or 4 days before they could get a flight. This now led to an acute labour shortage as there was no one to replace them.

Our company was starting to lose patience with the Iraqi market and I had to restrict my visit to 5 days and go and seek business in other parts of the Middle East. Moustafa understood and I promised to visit as often as I could even if it was only for a couple of days.

By October, on a very short visit, I found things even worse. Many factories had closed and others were using up the last of their stock. The UK was the only member of the EEC with a line of credit still open to Iraq. Half of a £250 million loan remained unused as did £50 million allocated to the Iraq pharmaceutical industry. So far, in order to keep this facility open, the Rafidain Bank had given special consideration to UK loans but repayments were only in sterling. No dollar payments were made because their reserves held in New York had run out.

The Bank of England had expressed concerns at the worsening situation and their representatives together with our minister of trade, Alan Clark, was due to visit Iraq in November for the international fair. Surprisingly, 60 British companies were going to exhibit.

Iraq was still insisting on a minimum of two year terms but had only reached agreement with countries in the Eastern Bloc, Korea and some Arab countries such as Egypt, Tunisia, Morocco and Jordan. Jordan however pulled out after only 5 months.

Iraq's other major trading partner, Turkey, with whom they did £1 billion of trade in 1985, took a long time to agree a new protocol for 1986. The agreement was only signed in September.

Iraq's negotiating position was now weaker than before and Turkey was able to secure better terms which meant that Turkish suppliers would get 77% immediately with the balance paid in instalments over two years.

Two large Japanese trading companies and several European organisations had closed their Baghdad offices and left the country. Ex pat workers, especially the Egyptians, were leaving in droves, with never-ending queues at the airport. Many shops had closed and there were shortages of basic foodstuffs such as sugar, cooking oil, detergents and soap powder. Factories making non essential items such as sweets, soft drinks, ice cream, yoghurt and snack foods were closed.

There was of course the World Cup to look forward to in Mexico. However the euphoria which followed Iraq's qualification soon evaporated as they were beaten by Mexico, Paraguay and Belgium, finishing bottom of their group, and failing to qualify for the knock out stages of the competition.

President Saddam Hussein however did not appear to be losing his grip over the war situation or public reaction. If anything he had increased his public appearances, hardly the way someone afraid for his life would act. There were unconfirmed reports of an attempted assassination at the beginning of September and it was rumoured that several Saddam look-a-likes had appeared, especially in the rural areas.

Iran had obtained Scud missiles, I believe from China, and was aiming these at Baghdad in retaliation for the bombing of Iranian towns. Two had been fired recently, evading the anti-missile system which had proved pretty useless. One landed in the Tigris but the other hit houses opposite the Meridian on the 20th September. Twenty-four people were killed and many more injured. Iraq continued to attack oil installations whilst at the United Nations all other Arab nations were pressing for a ceasefire, but with no success.

The Iranian response was to start attacking the oil tankers from Kuwait and the other Gulf States, which supported Iraq. This caused panic amongst the EEC, USA and USSR with the latter two offering to provide naval protection. The USA already had part of their fleet in the area and an air base at Dhahran in Saudi Arabia, so Kuwait accepted their offer.

Iraqi planes attacked one of the US escort vessels, the frigate "Stark" killing 38 men. The US called it a tragic mistake. Now that the USA had become involved, the situation was becoming even more complicated. Neither I nor the ordinary people of Iraq knew of all the twists and turns that were going on. In his excellent book; *Saddam Hussein, The Politics of Revenge* Said K. Aburish describes how the Americans managed to stop the flow of arms that were going to Iran from Israel. They used their reconnaissance aircraft, based at Dhahran, to survey Iranian key positions and this information was passed back to the Iraq military. The USA wanted this war over and done with because there was now a danger that the whole region could be drawn into it.

All in all it was a depressing picture and I did not go back again that year, as I had to spend more time in other markets. I had no option but to scale down my Iraq visits and in 1987 made only two fairly brief calls.

The first at the beginning of February was at a time when the pace of the war moved up several gears. It was now in its 7$^{th}$ year and conservative estimates stated that the numbers killed on both sides had now topped 1 million in a ratio of four Iranians to every Iraqi. This emphasised the failure of Iran's earlier human wave tactics and the appalling loss of life as a result. Iran's latest offensive however proved far more successful and provided the Iraq military with its sternest test yet.

The offensive, code named "Operation Kerbala" saw the Iranians break through four lines of defences protecting Basrah but they failed to penetrate the fifth. Basrah was now in easy shelling distance and suffered much damage and loss of life. All foreigners were evacuated from the area and many local people also left fearing that the city would fall into enemy hands.

Fortunately for the Iraq army, the wet weather which the Iranians had relied upon to neutralise Iraq's superiority in the air, did not materialise. The Iraqis were able to carry out countless air raids not only against the Iranian front line positions, but also far into

Iran attacking military, civilian and strategic economic targets. In return, Iran retaliated by firing more Scud missiles in the direction of Baghdad at the rate of two a week from the middle of January. Numbers 8 and 9 arrived during my stay. The Daura oil refinery south of the city seemed to be the main target, but unfortunately for people living in the surrounding area, the missiles fell short causing considerable damage and loss of life. I saw what was left of one street. For about 50 yards, houses had just disappeared and the rest of the street was a pile of rubble. Over 100 people had died here.

This latest escalation in the war was the final blow to Iraq's failing economy. With the austerity measures that took place in 1986 and with the price of oil starting to rise, it was hoped that, with a healthy increase in hard currency, a start could be made in clearing the backlog of debts in Europe. A schedule of repayments had been drawn up by the Iraq Central Bank. All these good intentions came to nought, as the war required extra funding. According to the various official bulletins issued during my stay, the Iraqi Air Force flew over 800 missions against Iranian targets. The cost of this alone must have been enormous.

The Government propaganda machine was working overtime. Nightly, on TV, were shown scenes of Iraqi "victories" and Iranian bodies in sickening detail. Large numbers of miserable looking prisoners of war were also shown and a separate channel was now being beamed at the Iranian public.

Pictures of Saddam Hussein now appeared everywhere again. He was shown as President/Field Marshal/tank commander/statesman/tribal chief/peasant/politician and father figure.

Privately, however, the people I met were greatly alarmed by these new developments. Many had sons aged 11 and 12 and saw the real prospect of them having to join the army at 17 for they saw no reason for the war to stop, convinced that Ayatollah Khomeini would go on for ever and never agree to a ceasefire.

Red and white taxis with roof racks carrying a body in a wooden crate were now a common sight. The crates were not always draped in an Iraqi flag now.

Few foreigners were now about and the Meridian was strangely quiet. I visited the British Embassy for their take on the situation and they didn't paint a very optimistic picture for the next six months anyway. There were some hopeful signs for later in the year. A new pipeline through Turkey was going to be opened in May increasing output by 500,000 barrels a day. The price of oil had now gone over $20 per barrel, which meant that, if OPEC did not curtail Iraq's production, income would reach at least $10 million a day. This would certainly ease things. A second pipeline through Saudi Arabia was also on schedule to be completed by the end of the year so despite everything there was a light at the end of the tunnel – maybe.

The rest of the Arab world had now been joined by other Islamic states in pressing for a resolution to be managed by the United Nations to bring the conflict to an end. Ayatollah Khomeini was having none of it and publicly declared that Iran would gain a complete victory by the end of March.

This seemed like a final throw of the dice, for I had been to a meeting at the department of trade and industry in London in January, when the commercial secretary from the British Embassy in Teheran told us that the Iranian economy had fallen apart, because of the lack of foreign exchange. He confirmed that the revenue from oil had fallen to a trickle because of Iraq's attacks on the installations at Kharg Island and elsewhere. The next three months were going to be critical for both sides.

It was to be the end of November before my next visit. During the summer months there had been a significant development in the war situation. The Kurdish separatists in the north backed by Iranian forces had made major inroads into Iraq and were a serious threat to the oil installations at Kirkuk. These attacks were dealt with, but what the West didn't know or chose to ignore, was *how*. Chemical weapons were used and thousands of Kurds and Iranians were killed. There then followed a policy of depopulating the far northern territories to deny the separatists any local support. People were moved to camps in the south of Iraq.

Iraq, too, had acquired a supply of rockets but unlike the Iranian ones, these were long range and fitted with chemical warheads, could be aimed at targets well inside Iran. Teheran was now in reach and suffered greatly

Revenue from oil exports was being diverted straight into the war effort and there was little sign of any improvement in the repayment schedules. It was being reported that Syria wanted to improve its relations with Iraq. Up until now they had seemed to favour Iran, but with the perceived threat to oil supplies from the Gulf they were now offering Iraq the opportunity to open the old pipeline in exchange for oil. The significance of this would be felt in the Lebanon where Syria had backed pro-Iranian groups. Iran would now be totally isolated amongst all the Middle East countries.

People I spoke to seemed pleased that the USA had got involved and felt that at last an end to fighting might be in sight. This mood of cautious optimism was being reflected in the plans being discussed with local businessmen, to transfer public utility and food processing industries into private hands. A new minister of industry had been appointed to restructure Iraqi industry as soon as the war was over.

Circumstances prevented me from going to Iraq until September 1988. By this time the war had ended. The manner of its ending perhaps hid one of the most infamous acts of modern times, which was only revealed later. Because of American involvement in the northern Gulf, Iran's efforts were being neutralised. Their occupation of Fao was being blockaded so, once again, they turned their attention to the north where the Americans could not reach them.

The Kurds in the north were trying to mount further attacks. Saddam Hussein's response was to attack with chemical weapons and the massacre of men, women and children at Halabja will remain a stain on Iraq's history. In the south, an Iraqi offensive using rockets and yet more chemical weapons, drove the Iranians out of Iraqi territory and there was a possibility that their own territory would once again be occupied.

These events finally persuaded the Iranian religious leaders that no purpose could now be achieved by continuing the war. The fact that

America was involved now gave them the excuse to say that it was the hand of Satan that had beaten them and not Saddam.

United Nations Resolution 598 was signed on the 18th July 1988. The war had taken over a million lives and had cost Iraq $65 billion dollars.

Two months later, the euphoria following Iran's acceptance of the UN Resolution, was still very evident in post war Baghdad. There was a buzz of excitement and energy about the place, in sharp contrast to the deep depression, which settled in as the eight year old war dragged on.

The streets were packed with people. There were endless traffic jams. Open air cafés, restaurants and nightclubs were doing a roaring trade and staying open until the early hours of the morning. Pleasure craft had returned to the Tigris – hitherto a high security zone – and at night the boats were brilliantly lit by coloured lights.

Saddam Hussein hailed the ceasefire and the Iranian decision to accept UN Resolution 598 as a victory for Iraq and a surrender by Iran. Iraq TV continuously showed film of captured Iranian soldiers and masses of equipment seized in the last few days of fighting before the ceasefire.

After all the "victory" parades had ended, it was perhaps time to analyse the end result. Iraq's claim that they were victorious could only be justified by the fact that they had successfully defended their territory but perhaps more importantly, had stopped the advance of fundamental Islam. It had been Ayatollah Khomeini's aim to topple the Iraq regime and in particular Saddam Hussein. Whilst Iran now faced internal turmoil and a leadership struggle, Saddam Hussein's position was stronger than ever.

Peace talks were set to take place and considering the animosity between the two sides, these were not expected to conclude rapidly.

In the press and on TV, the Government were promising the Iraqi people "good times" ahead. Following the ceasefire, stockpiles of consumer goods were released into the market and the population went on a spending spree. Shortages of basic foodstuffs and everyday items soon returned and I made a note in my diary that the toilet paper in the hotel was like sandpaper!

A new commercial TV station had been opened although the adverts seemed to be restricted to restaurants, night clubs and fashion shops.

My customers were eagerly waiting for the chance to resume business and were already formulating their plans. They knew, as well as I did, that normal trading conditions would be a while coming yet.

The overriding problem was the national debt. Fifty per cent was owed to Arab countries and it was widely expected that this debt would be cancelled in gratitude for halting Khomeini's plans for a totally fundamental Islamic Middle East.

For the rest there appeared to be two options:-

Firstly, that the Arab banks would now lend Iraq the funds to clear outstanding debts. Such a loan would be interest free. Secondly, bearing in mind Iraq's potential as a future market or, foreign banks would allow a further rescheduling of payments in return for long term agreements on trade.

A visit to the commercial section at the British Embassy confirmed my suspicions that normality was a long way off. This was further confirmed when I managed to get an appointment with the Rafidain Bank to check on the progress or otherwise of some payments that were due to our company. The comments that were made did not fill me with confidence and I had to tell Moustafa that 1989 did not look to be a good year for us.

An amnesty had been granted to all economic and political prisoners serving sentences up to 15 years. Demobilisation of the army had begun slowly. Men aged between 45 and 55 were gradually returning to civilian life. The problem now was that there was little in the way of employment for them despite the fact that 2,000 Egyptian workers a week were being repatriated.

Another "black cloud" hovered over the situation in that the full horror of the chemical attack on the Kurds at Halabja had been discovered and a bitter exchange had broken out between Iraq and the US. Things came to a head on the day I left Baghdad when massive anti-American demonstrations were organised. The American ambassador had only been in Iraq for two years and now relations had gone from good to bad very quickly after the end of the war. The situation had become so bad that the US was considering sanctions and my concern was that the UK could be drawn into the row, and harm the good relations, which existed. If I had known then the full story of Halabja, I would have felt differently. Even so my opinion would be to condemn Saddam's regime, not the Iraqi people.

All in all, it was a volatile situation still. It was difficult to persuade people that "good times" would not happen over night. The wave of optimism was reflected in the number of marriages taking place. Thursday evenings used to be the time when wedding parties arrived for receptions at the major hotels. Now every night seemed to be wedding night and from early evening the hotels were besieged by wedding groups which were very noisy because of people playing trumpets, beating drums, dancing, shouting and singing. Maybe a population explosion would occur in 1989!

# 16

## THE EVIL THAT MEN DO, LIVES AFTER THEM
SHAKESPEARE – JULIUS CAESAR

The information that I was getting from Moustafa at the beginning of 1989 was not encouraging, so it was no surprise when I went at the end of February, to find that the euphoria, which followed the declaration of peace, had completely disappeared. It had been replaced by a mood of frustration caused by the length of time it was taking to get things back to normal in relation to supplies and ordinary foodstuffs. Even the goods that were available were of very poor quality.

President Saddam Hussein was now, as had become very apparent during the war, running a one-man show. He had decreed that top priority be given to the reconstruction of Basrah.

Iraq's oil revenue was now back to its pre-war level but it was being channelled into Basrah's recovery. It was felt that the main reason for this decision was to maintain the support of the largely Shi'ite south, vital if he was to keep control over the whole country.

Relations with Jordan had turned nasty again. In the previous 12 months the value of the Iraqi Dinar had fallen steadily against all hard currencies. It had also lost value against all the major Arab currencies, with the exception of the Jordanian Dinar, which was being dragged down to the same level. Considerable friction now existed between Iraq and Jordan and high level attempts were being made to patch up the differences and to sign a new protocol agreement, which would protect the Jordanian Dinar and allow Jordanian manufacturers and growers to start exporting to Iraq again. The situation ended in chaos at the end of 1988 when all trading was suspended. It was alleged that many Jordanian companies were breaking the rules regarding the country of origin and simply using Jordan as a transit route for foreign goods.

My regular visit to the British Embassy did not give me any scope for optimism and they, quite rightly, predicted that Iraq's economic recovery was going to take a long time. International debt repayments were falling further behind.

Our customers were equally frustrated but of course under Saddam's regime, criticism was voiced privately not publicly. Some had already signed up to taking on some of the State owned factories but now could not take matters further.

I waited throughout the rest of 1989 for the green shoots of recovery to appear, but none were forthcoming. At the beginning of 1990 I was visiting other areas in the Middle East and decided to make another short visit to Baghdad to try and see if any improvement was on the horizon. My managing director accompanied me on the Iraq section. Our company was still owed a considerable amount from delayed payments and he wanted to get a first hand report from the Rafidain Bank and the British Embassy. Neither gave any reason for optimism.

On the final day before he left me in Baghdad, he expressed a wish to visit Babylon. Moustafa drove us to the site, which had not changed in the 15 years since my first visit. That is with one exception. On an adjoining site, a reconstruction of King Nebuchadnezzar's Palace was being built by command of Saddam Hussein. Each brick in the building was inscribed with the name of Saddam Hussein. He was following the same philosophy as King Nebuchadnezzar. Thinking back, it is ironic that their two empires ended in ruins.

As usual on all my visits to Iraq, I was warmly welcomed by all and shown much hospitality in very trying circumstances. I was not to know of course, that this would be my last visit. Moustafa was keen to get going again but all our customer visits ended with the same negative result. Fortunately for him, his textile business was largely based with Turkish companies, so the same restrictions did not apply.

What none of us knew then was that Saddam Hussein had his sights firmly set on Kuwait. In the 12 months since the war with Iran had finished, any funds which hadn't been used in the reconstruction of Basrah, had been used to re-equip the army. The repayment of outstanding debts had been pushed well into the background. Kuwait, Iraq's ally during the war, was accused of the over-production of oil. Saddam Hussein stated that this was having a detrimental effect on Iraq's recovery programme. I think the West thought that this spat would be sorted out by OPEC and what had not been anticipated, was that Saddam Hussein would order the invasion of Kuwait on August 2nd 1990. This small state was quickly overrun.

There was universal condemnation and an immediate trade embargo imposed. The UK Government led by Mrs. Thatcher, immediately froze all Iraq assets in the UK including the branch of the Rafidain Bank in London. This ruined any possible chance of British companies receiving payments, some of which had been filtering through, albeit slowly. Our company was still owed £500,000.

So my Iraq "adventure" was over. All the hard work and entrepreneurial skills of our customers now counted for nothing as Iraq became a pariah state.

The first Gulf war was a disaster for Iraq as thousands more were killed and the military equipment bought in 1989 was largely destroyed. After Iraq's withdrawal from Kuwait, the decision not to pursue the retreating army to Baghdad has often been questioned.

Similarly the lack of support for the Shia uprising in the south meant that Saddam had just about enough resources left to crush it.
The continued threat of Iraq's chemical warfare capability and a perceived nuclear threat were still giving the UN a massive headache. UN sanctions were tightened and these were to last virtually until the next Gulf war. It was the poor people of Iraq who suffered not Saddam. Medical facilities were hardest hit.

Even though UN inspection teams confirmed that Iraq's chemical and nuclear warfare capability had been dismantled by 1993, sanctions were not eased.

Strangely this situation seemed to strengthen Saddam Hussein's position, as he was now perceived by many in the Arab world as standing up to the might of America and the UN.

I kept in touch with Moustafa by letter. Our correspondence was largely about our respective families and we did not comment on the ongoing situation as I thought censorship might be in place.
History will judge Saddam Hussein. It will also judge George W. Bush and Tony Blair and all the faceless individuals who fed them the information on which they based their decisions.

Iraq's troubled history continues and I feel so sorry for this beautiful, historic country and its wonderful people who have been so badly betrayed.

Although in the 15 years I had been visiting, I had been to many historical sites, there were many more that I would have liked to have seen. Ur, for example, dating back 6,000 years and its famous holy ziggurat temple. Najaf, Kufa, Nippur, Uruk are all in the south whilst in the north the countryside beyond Mosul is said to be very spectacular.

I gradually lost contact with all my friends there including Moustafa. Shortly after the end of the second Gulf war he contacted me by mobile telephone to say that it was too dangerous for him to go to his office in central Baghdad, and he would try and work from his home. I have heard nothing since and all my letters have remained unanswered. I just hope he and his family are alive. Khalid and his family emigrated and the last time I heard, were living in Canada.

Has Iraq got a future? The answer is most definitely yes, but, it can only be decided by the Iraqis themselves. The sooner all foreign troops leave, the better. That includes all those extremists who have descended on Iraq to fight as well as Al Qaeda. The make up of Iraq's population is too diverse for it ever to be totally Islamic state like Iran. That diversity is its strength.

It is 33 years since I first went to Iraq. Then its constitution allowed religious freedom, free education and health care for all and its economy was being allowed to drive forward at such a pace that self-sufficiency was a realistic aim. If it can get back to this position with a fully representative elected assembly, then I feel all will work out. This may be a too simplistic view and at the back of my mind I have to wonder if the divisions between the Shia and Sunni and Kurdish communities are now too deep for them to be reconciled. Only time will tell but the Iraqi people have to be given the opportunity to find out without outside interference.

I see from the internet, that our best customer, Mr Abdul Wahab Al Bunnia is all set to re-launch his companies. He is now chairman of the Bunnia Group and four of his sons are managing directors. Thinking back to the 70s, his companies set the standards which others followed. I hope he can do it again.

Perhaps I could end my tale with two verses from one of the poems of the US poet, Longfellow.

> Trust no future, howe'er pleasant.
> Let the dead past bury the dead.
> Act, act in the living present.
> Heart within, and God o'erhead.
>
> Lives of great men all remind us
> We can make our lives sublime,
> And, departing leave behind us
> Footprints in the sands of time.

# ACKNOWLEDGEMENTS

1. Ron Wilcox, *Battles on the Tigris*, Pen & Sword Military.
2. Said K Aburish, *Saddam Hussein, The Politics of Revenge*, Bloomsbury.
3. D.C. Browning, *Dictionary of Quotations*, J.M. Dent.
4. Wikipedia, The Free Encyclopedia.
5. The Keep Military Museum, Dorchester.
6. The National Archives, Kew.
7. The British Museum, Babylon Exhibition.
8. Commonwealth War Graves Commission, Maidenhead.
9. Authorised and New English versions of The Bible.
10. *Iraq Tourist Guide Book 1982*.
11. vin Young, *Return to the Marshes*, Futura.
12. Pete Seeger & Joe Hickerson.
13. *Iraq in Pictures*, Sterling Publishing.
14. The Baghdad Observer.
15. The Arab Times.
16. The Arab News.
17. The Kuwaiti Times.
18. The Iraq Ministry of Telecommunications and Post.
19. My grateful thanks to my son Michael for the formatting of this book and getting it ready for publication.